From Our House to Yours

curried
Pumpkin Soup

From Our House to Yours

COMFORT FOOD TO GIVE AND SHARE

A Cookbook to Benefit Meals On Wheels of San Francisco

FOREWORD BY JOYCE GOLDSTEIN
PHOTOGRAPHS BY E. J. ARMSTRONG
Compiled by the Editors of Chronicle Books

CHRONICLE BOOKS
SAN FRANCISCO

ACKNOWLEDGMENTS

Chronicle Books would like to thank all of our cookbook writers, whose recipes provide such comforting food for our families and friends. We would also like to thank our terrific group of copy editors, designers, and photographers, who have helped us to create our beautiful books.

Library of Congress Cataloging-in-Publication Data:

From our house to yours : comfort food to give and share : a book to benefit Meals On Wheels of San Francisco/ compiled and edited by the editors of Chronicle Books ; foreword by Joyce Goldstein.
    p. cm.
Includes index.
 1. Cookery. 2. Gifts. I. Chronicle Books (Firm)
 TX715 .F876547 2002
 641.5—dc21
                                        2001008499
ISBN 0-8118-3691-6

Manufactured in China

Prop stylist: Kim Holderman
Food stylists: Diana Isaiou and Patty Wittmann
Photo Assistant and life saver: Scott Pitts
Design: Gretchen Scoble Design

Distributed in Canada by Raincoast Books
9050 Shaughnessy Street
Vancouver, BC V6P 6E5

10 9 8 7 6 5 4 3

Chronicle Books LLC
85 Second Street
San Francisco, California 94105
www.chroniclebooks.com

Table of Contents

Chapter 4: Salads and Sides

Chapter 5: Sweets

Chapter 6: Healing Tonics and Elixirs

Foreword

BY JOYCE GOLDSTEIN

Food has the power to heal, to comfort, and to convey care and affection. Although my son, Evan, is now a grown man with children of his own, one of my most poignant comfort-food memories is associated with his birth. My friend Eve Pell, who had given birth to her son, Daniel, six months previously, was not someone whose life revolved around food and cooking as mine did. However, on the day that I came home from the hospital, she appeared at my doorstep with a dozen peanut-butter-and-jelly sandwiches. Those sandwiches saved me from starvation while I was coping with sleep deprivation and learning how to nurse a newborn. Her thoughtful gift comforted me and kept me nourished until I got into the routine of motherhood.

When my dear friend Barbara Tropp was in the hospital recuperating after surgery, I called her to arrange a visit. She said, "Oh, Joycie, the food is so bad, I cannot eat it. Will you please bring me something with flavor?" I ran to the market, bought some tender fish, raced home, and prepared couscous and baked the fish with Moroccan herbs and spices and lots of love. As I entered her room, just the aroma seemed to lift her spirits. Nurses and a few ambulatory patients peeked in and asked, "What is that yummy smell?" We reheated the dish in the hospital microwave and Barbara ate for the first time in days.

When someone is temporarily incapacitated, or recuperating from surgery, and can't get to the market or is unable to cook, there is no better gift than homey food and a visit. A container of a favorite soup, a savory stew, some sandwiches on good bread, a quiche, or potpie can brighten the day and hasten a recovery. After the death of a loved one, the grieving family truly feels cared for by friends who bring casseroles, soups, pies, and other covered dishes to sustain them until they are able to return to day-to-day life. But what happens when chronic illness or the advancing frailties of age put an end to normal domestic routine? People may be so physically challenged that they are unable to get to a market. Many are isolated from family and friends and have no one to shop for them. They run the risk of malnutrition and are dependent upon the kindness of others for their everyday sustenance.

Fortunately, many homebound elderly are visited daily by Meals On Wheels. The combination of the hot

food and genial conversation with the driver may be the brightest moment of their day. Meals On Wheels also provides social-work services and nutrition counseling for their clients. Presently the San Francisco organization delivers two nutritionally balanced meals a day to 1,500 seniors. As our senior population increases, the need for Meals On Wheels will grow exponentially; the organization's resources, however, are already stretched to the maximum. Meals On Wheels depends upon community support and donations to supplement government grants. Proceeds from the sale of this book will benefit this worthy organization. These well-chosen recipes are fine examples of food that offer comfort along with delicious flavors and nutrition. All that is needed to complete the equation are your hands to provide the craft and your heart to provide the care and the love.

Introduction

As the saying goes, when the going gets tough, the cooks get cooking. In times of transition and change, there is nothing more cheering and healing than the gift of homemade food. Everyone knows the curative powers of hot chicken soup, the comfort found in a swirl of mashed potatoes, and the sweet bliss of a chocolate brownie. These are dishes people crave in times of need.

Here is a collection of recipes to suit every taste and hour. Chosen from some of our favorite cookbooks, these recipes will help you find the perfect dish to make for friends who need some special attention. Pick from among four different chicken soups for a relative who's feeling under the weather. Make a simple lasagna for a sleep-deprived couple with a baby just home from the hospital. Carry a batch of chocolate chip cookies warm from the oven to new neighbors who have yet to unpack their house.

Some recipes can be made ahead of time, and others can be made in a hurry. Many make enough for leftovers and some can be easily frozen. We've included recipes for the whole family, grown-ups and kids, meat eaters and vegetarians. You'll find recipes for soothing soups; comforting casseroles; flavorful braises and roasts; wonderful vegetables; and sumptuous sweets that can be transported with care. To make the trip even smoother, whenever possible, we've provided tips on preparing dishes in advance and reheating them.

Although this book is organized by course, craving is the guiding principle. It is a great idea to find out your friend's cravings (as well as their dislikes) so that you can make just the right food for them to have on hand.

We have tried to pick a range of tasty recipes from our large list of Chronicle cookbooks to send from our house to yours. We hope that this collection makes cooking to give and share as comforting to you as the dishes you make are to your friends.

BRINGING FOOD TO FRIENDS

With the exception of some of the cookies and the tea blends, which can be sent by mail, most of the dishes in this book are best given in person. In fact, part of the joy of giving food can be spending time together enjoying it.

One of the easiest ways to transport food is in the vessel in which it was cooked. Casseroles, for example, are easily carried covered, in the dish in which they were baked. Soups, however, are better cooled and poured into plastic containers with tight-fitting lids suitable for reheating in the microwave or for transferring into pots upon arrival. You can include the containers as part of your gift, or a piece of tape with your name stuck on the bottom of a container or plate will help you to retrieve it later.

If you want to cook for, and perhaps eat with, your friend, prepare the dish up to the point of cooking and bring it in as many plastic containers as needed. You can use your friend's cooking utensils and then stay to wash them and put them away. Restaurant-supply houses are a great source for a variety of plastic storage containers with tight-fitting lids.

To transport food in its cooking vessel hot from your kitchen so that it can be eaten the moment it arrives, line a cardboard box with several layers of newspaper. Cover the vessel with a lid or aluminum foil, wrap it in newspapers and a heavy towel, and place it in the box. This will keep any food fairly hot for up to an hour. You can also make most of the dishes in this book ahead of time, to reheat yourself or to leave for your friend to reheat. Most prepared foods, hot or cold, including those containing meat, can be safely kept at room temperature for up to 2 hours.

If you want to bring an extra gift for your friend, wrap the food container in a beautiful kitchen towel or napkin, put it in a gift basket along with a serving plate or bowl, and tuck in a bouquet of flowers, too, if you like. In this case, be sure to include a note with instructions for reheating and perhaps freezing the dish.

CHAPTER 1

Simple Soups

Hot soup soothes the soul. Whether you prefer your chicken soup with noodles or matzo balls, rice noodles or coconut milk, you will find a version here to help cure a friend's cold. Minestrone and miso soups will please vegetarian and vegan friends, and white bean soup and beef and barley soup will satisfy hearty eaters.

The key to great soup is good stock. If possible keep home-made stock on hand in your freezer for making soup on the spur of the moment. If you don't have a chicken stock recipe, use Maryana Vollstedt's stock recipe for Chicken Soup for the Soul (page 16). For a fabulous vegetable stock, see the broth variation of Rick Rodger's vegetable soup (page 22). Of course, you can also purchase frozen stock or low-fat low-sodium broth as a good substitute.

Most soups will keep, covered, in the refrigerator for up to 3 days, or can be frozen in plastic freezer containers, for up to 3 months. (Fish soups do not store well.) Reheat soups over low heat, stirring frequently and adding more liquid if necessary.

Chicken Soup for the Soul
(CHICKEN NOODLE SOUP)

Chicken soup from Maryana Vollstedt's Big Book of Soups & Stews *is just what the doctor ordered! Luscious egg noodles transform a simple chicken stock by into a soulful concoction with the power to heal. You can use the stock, without the noodles, as an ingredient in other dishes in this book.* ❤ SERVES 6

Stock:

1 chicken (3 to $3\frac{1}{2}$ pounds), quartered

10 cups water

1 yellow onion, quartered

3 carrots, each cut into 4 pieces

2 celery stalks, including some tops, cut up

2 garlic cloves, halved

3 parsley sprigs

3 to 4 fresh basil leaves, or $\frac{1}{2}$ teaspoon dried basil

1 teaspoon dried thyme

$1\frac{1}{2}$ teaspoons salt

1 teaspoon peppercorns

1 bay leaf

$\frac{1}{4}$ cup dry white wine (optional)

2 cups (4 ounces) dried egg noodles

1. To make the stock: In a large soup pot, combine the chicken, water, vegetables, and garlic. Bring to a boil. Skim off the foam. Add the parsley, basil, thyme, salt, peppercorns, bay leaf, and wine, if using. Reduce heat to medium-low, cover, and simmer until the chicken is very tender, 1 to 1½ hours. Transfer the chicken to a plate and let cool. Strain the stock into a bowl and discard the solids. Using a fat separator, degrease the stock and return to the pot or, if time allows, refrigerate it overnight and then remove the congealed fat.

2. Remove the skin and bones from the chicken and discard. Cut the chicken into bite-sized pieces and add 2 to 3 cups chicken pieces to the stock (use the remainder for other purposes). Add the noodles and bring to a boil. Reduce heat to medium-low and cook, uncovered, until the noodles are tender, about 10 minutes. Taste and adjust the seasoning.

TO MAKE AHEAD: Let cool, cover, and refrigerate for up to 3 days, or freeze before adding the noodles in an airtight container for up to 2 months.

TO REHEAT: If frozen, let thaw in the refrigerator before reheating. Bring to a simmer over low heat. Cook the noodles separately in boiling salted water until tender, about 10 minutes. Drain and add to the simmering soup.

Chicken Soup with Matzo Balls

When it comes to healthful food, nothing beats chicken soup with matzo balls—at least according to authors Jeannette Ferrary and Louise Fiszer in A Good Day for Soup. *Recipes for chicken soup may be infinite, but there seem to be only two types of matzo balls: lead balloons and feather-light floaters. The ones that follow are in the latter category, with a tasty twist on tradition in the addition of fresh herbs. This soup is best made with a rich homemade stock.* ♥ SERVES 6

Matzo Balls:

2 eggs

2 tablespoons melted chicken fat, margarine, or vegetable oil

¼ cup chicken stock (page 16)

½ cup matzo meal

¼ teaspoon salt

1 tablespoon *each* chopped fresh flat-leaf parsley, dill, and chives

8 cups chicken stock, preferably clarified, or low-sodium broth

1. To make the matzo ball dough: In a large bowl, beat the eggs with the chicken fat, margarine, or oil and stock until well blended. Stir in the matzo meal, salt, and herbs. Cover and refrigerate for 1 hour.

2. Bring a large pot of salted water to a boil. With wet hands, form matzo balls about 1 inch in diameter. Do not compact them. Drop in the boiling water. When the balls float to the surface, reduce heat to a bare simmer, cover, and cook for about 35 minutes. Remove with a slotted spoon, cover, and refrigerate until ready to use.

3. To serve, place the stock in a large pot, add the matzo balls and simmer over low heat until warm.

TO MAKE AHEAD: Let the matzo balls cool completely, cover, and refrigerate for up to 3 days.

TO REHEAT: Proceed with Step 3.

Thai Chicken-Coconut Soup with Galanga
(TOME KHA GAI)

This extraordinary soup by Nancie McDermott from her book Real Thai *is rich with coconut milk and sharp with the vibrant Asian flavors of galanga, lemongrass, and lime leaves. Galanga, a member of the ginger family, has a strong citrus flavor. Galanga is available frozen in many Southeast Asian markets, as are kaffir lime leaves.* ❤ SERVES 6 TO 8

1 whole boneless, skinless chicken breast

2 boneless, skinless chicken thighs

4 fresh lemongrass stalks

$4\frac{1}{2}$ cups coconut milk

$1\frac{1}{2}$ cups chicken stock (page 16) or low-sodium broth

20 quarter-sized slices fresh, frozen, or dried galanga

12 fresh kaffir lime leaves

1 cup sliced fresh mushrooms

2 tablespoons fish sauce

2 tablespoons fresh lime juice

2 green onions, sliced thin

2 tablespoons chopped fresh cilantro

1. Cut the chicken breast and thighs into large bite-sized pieces; set aside.

2. Cut away the grassy tops of the lemongrass stalks, leaving stalks about 6 inches long. Cut away any hard root section to leave a clean, smooth, flat base below the bulb. Remove and discard tough outer leaves. Using the blunt edge of a cleaver or the back of a heavy knife, bruise each stalk, whacking it firmly at 2-inch intervals and rolling it over to bruise the stalk on all sides. Cut each stalk crosswise into 4 pieces; set aside.

3. In a large saucepan, combine the coconut milk and chicken stock or broth and bring to a gentle boil over medium-high heat. Stir in the lemongrass, chicken, galanga, and 6 of the lime leaves. Reduce heat to a simmer and cook until the chicken is done, about 10 minutes.

4. Add the mushrooms and remove from heat. Stir in the fish sauce, lime juice, green onions, cilantro, and remaining lime leaves. Taste and add more fish sauce and lime juice if you like. Serve hot.

NOTE: Thai cooks usually leave the herbs in the soup, even though they aren't edible. If you like, strain the soup before adding the mushrooms to remove the lemongrass, galanga, and lime leaves. Then return the soup and chicken to the pan, and add the remaining ingredients.

TO MAKE AHEAD: When chicken is cooked, let the soup cool completely, cover, and refrigerate for up to 2 days. To complete the soup, reheat gently and stir in the mushrooms, fish sauce, lime leaves, lime juice, green onions, and cilantro. Freeze in an airtight container for up to 2 months.

TO REHEAT: If frozen, let thaw in the refrigerator. Reheat gently over medium-low heat, adding some green onions, cilantro, and lime juice to brighten the flavor.

Asian Chicken Noodle Soup

Vibrant with colorful vegetables, this light Asian chicken noodle soup by Sam Gugino from Low-Fat Cooking to Beat the Clock *is perfect for friends who like a brothy soup. It goes together so quickly, you can make it for a last-minute gift. The secret ingredient is fish sauce, which is available at Asian markets and many supermarkets.* ♥ SERVES 4

$5\frac{1}{2}$ cups low-fat chicken stock (page 16) or fat-free
    low-sodium broth

$\frac{1}{2}$ cup rice wine or dry sherry

2 ounces rice noodles (rice sticks)

Canola oil spray

One 2-inch piece fresh ginger

1 bunch green onions

4 ounces shiitake mushrooms or button mushrooms, sliced

8 ounces boneless, skinless chicken breasts or chicken tenders

12 ounces bok choy (preferably baby bok choy) or napa cabbage

8 ounces mung bean sprouts

One 8-ounce can sliced water chestnuts

2 tablespoons fish sauce

Salt and freshly ground pepper to taste

1 tablespoon Asian sesame oil

1. Put the chicken stock or broth and rice wine in a large saucepan. Cover and put over high heat. Run the hot water tap while you break the noodles in half. Put the noodles in a medium bowl and cover with hot tap water; set aside.

2. Spray a large, nonstick sauté pan with canola oil spray and put over medium heat. Peel and halve the ginger. With the motor of a food processor running, drop the ginger down the chute and finely chop. Trim the bulb ends of the green onions. Remove the green parts and set aside. Put the white parts into the food processor and pulse just until chopped. Add the ginger and onion mixture to the sauté pan, raise the heat to high, and stir.

3. Remove the stems from the shiitake mushrooms (leave the stems on if using button mushrooms) and thinly slice the caps. Add the mushrooms to the sauté pan and stir. Cut the chicken into ½-inch cubes. Add the chicken to the sauté pan and stir. As soon as the chicken stock mixture has come to a boil, add it to the sauté pan and stir well. Cover and bring to a boil over high heat.

4. Cut the tops of the bok choy or cabbage crosswise into ½-inch-wide ribbons. As you go farther down to the thicker stem, cut strips ¼ inch wide. Discard the bottom ½ inch. Drain the noodles. When the soup has returned to a boil, add the bok choy, noodles, and bean sprouts. Cover and return to a boil, about 1 minute.

5. Meanwhile, open and drain the can of water chestnuts. Add the water chestnuts, fish sauce, salt, and pepper. Stir, cover, and cook for 2 minutes or until the noodles are tender. Finely chop the green parts of the onions. Remove the soup from heat. Stir in the sesame oil. Serve sprinkled with the green onions.

TO MAKE AHEAD: Prepare through Step 5 except for adding the chopped green onions and sesame oil. Let cool completely, cover, and refrigerate for up to 2 days.

TO REHEAT: Bring to a simmer over low heat. Stir in the sesame oil and sprinkly with green onions to serve.

Old-Fashioned Vegetable-Rice Soup

Rick Rodgers keeps quarts of this flavorful vegetarian soup in his freezer so that he is always ready for a friend in need. This soup from his book On Rice *is almost hearty, although one of its beauties is its light, but flavorful, simplicity. You can cook the rice right in the soup, but Rick recommends preparing it separately so you can add as much rice as you want. And by putting on a separate pot of grains, you can use whichever you prefer, from amaranth to wheat berries. Without rice, the soup can be strained for use as a vegetable stock in other recipes. If you like, make a double batch, serving half as soup and straining the remainder for stock.* ♥ SERVES 6

1 onion, chopped

1 celery stalk with leaves, chopped

1 carrot, chopped

8 large garlic cloves, crushed

2 parsley sprigs

1 bay leaf

$\frac{1}{4}$ teaspoon dried thyme

$\frac{1}{2}$ teaspoon salt, plus more to taste

$\frac{1}{4}$ teaspoon freshly ground pepper, plus more to taste

$1\frac{1}{2}$ quarts water, or more as needed

1 large waxy new potato, scrubbed and cut into $\frac{1}{4}$-inch dice

Rice or other grain for serving, prepared according to
   package instructions

Chopped fresh herbs, such as basil, dill, or tarragon,
   for garnish

1. In a large pot, combine all of the ingredients except the potato, rice, and herbs. Add more water if needed to completely cover the vegetables. Bring to a boil over high heat, reduce the heat to low, and partially cover. Simmer very gently for 1 hour. Add the potato and cook until the stock is well flavored and the vegetables are tender, about 30 minutes more. Season with salt and pepper.

2. To serve, spoon rice into individual soup bowls, ladle the soup over the rice, and sprinkle with the herbs.

VARIATION: HOMEMADE VEGETABLE STOCK
Prepare the soup through Step 1. Pour it through a coarse-mesh sieve set over a large bowl. Discard the solids in the sieve. Let cool to room temperature. Cover and refrigerate for up to 3 days, or freeze for up to 3 months. Makes about 6 cups.

TO MAKE AHEAD: Prepare through Step 1. Let cool completely, cover, and refrigerate for up to 3 days, or freeze in an airtight container for up to 2 months.

TO REHEAT: If frozen, let thaw in the refrigerator. Bring to a simmer over low heat. Proceed with Step 2.

Minestrone Romano "a Crudo"
("RAW" MINESTRONE, ROMAN STYLE)

The secret to the success of this spectacularly colorful soup from The Vegetarian Table: Italy *by Julia della Croce is the use of uncompromisingly fresh vegetables, good-quality extra-virgin olive oil, and authentic Parmigiano-Reggiano cheese. In the nonvegetarian version of this soup, a large meaty ham bone or ham hock is included. Another method for giving a boost of flavor is the Ligurian style of stirring in a few tablespoons of pesto just before serving. This recipe makes enough for ten people, so you may want to divide up the batch to give to more than one friend, or simply plan on having a batch for yourself.* ❤ SERVES 10

3 tablespoons extra-virgin olive oil,
   plus additional olive oil for the table

3 canned plum tomatoes, seeded and chopped,
   plus ¼ cup of their juices

1 large onion, chopped coarsely

1 potato, peeled and diced

1 large celery stalk with leaves, stalk thinly sliced
   and leaves chopped

¾ pound butternut squash, diced (about 1½ cups)

2 teaspoons plus 3 tablespoons minced fresh rosemary,
   or 1 teaspoon plus 2 tablespoons dried rosemary

3 tablespoons minced fresh flat-leaf parsley leaves and
   stems, plus 3 tablespoons chopped fresh flat-leaf parsley

1 large carrot, peeled and diced

½ pound green cabbage, finely shredded (about 1½ cups)

1 pound fresh cranberry beans, shelled (about 1 cup) or
   2 cups canned pinto or pink beans, drained and rinsed

3 quarts water

2 tablespoons salt, or to taste

Freshly ground pepper to taste

¼ pound green beans, cut into 1-inch lengths (about 1 cup)

2 small zucchini, cut into ½-inch-thick slices

1½ cups cauliflower florets

1 cup conchigliette ("little shells") or ditalini
   ("little thimbles") pasta

4 large garlic cloves, finely chopped

Freshly grated Parmesan cheese, preferably
   Parmigiano-Reggiano

continued

1. In a large pot, combine the 3 tablespoons oil, tomatoes and juice, onion, potato, celery, squash, the 2 teaspoons fresh or 1 teaspoon dried rosemary, the 3 tablespoons minced parsley, the carrot, cabbage, fresh cranberry beans (reserve canned beans, if using), water, salt, and pepper. Cover the pot and bring to a boil over high heat. Immediately reduce heat to medium-low, cover with the lid askew, and simmer for about 40 minutes, or until the beans and vegetables are tender.

2. Add the green beans, zucchini, cauliflower, and pasta; cook for 8 minutes. Stir in the garlic, the 3 tablespoons fresh rosemary or 2 tablespoons dried rosemary, and the 3 tablespoons chopped parsley; if using cooked beans, add them at this point. Continue cooking the soup, uncovered, over medium heat, until the pasta is al dente (it will not remain so, since it soaks in the hot soup, so it is best to undercook it somewhat), about 8 minutes.

3. Serve the soup with abundant freshly grated Parmesan, a dribble of olive oil, and freshly ground pepper.

NOTES: There are infinite variations on the theme of minestrone, which means, literally, "big soup." These reflect regional cooking styles as well as availability of ingredients. In summer, almost any vegetable in season might be used in minestrone, including other summer squash varieties, Swiss chard, peas, fava beans, carrots, and celery. In winter, cabbage, dried beans, and cold-weather vegetables such as cabbages predominate.

If you like, 1 cup dried beans can be substituted for the fresh cranberry beans or canned beans. To use dried cranberry beans, rinse and pick over 1 cup beans, then soak in water to cover for 4 hours or up to overnight. Drain and combine with ½ teaspoon salt and water to cover in a large saucepan. Bring to a boil, skim off any foam that rises to the top, and reduce the heat to low. Simmer very gently for 1 to 1½ hours.

TO MAKE AHEAD: Prepare through Step 2. Let cool completely, cover, and refrigerate, covered, for up to 5 days. Freeze in an airtight container for up to 2 months.

TO REHEAT: Bring to a simmer over low heat. Proceed with Step 3 to serve.

Shiitake, Miso, and Barley Soup

With its meaty chunks of shiitake and the creamy texture of barley, this Asian-inspired vegan version of a traditional eastern European soup from Lorna Sass's New Soy Cookbook *will warm you on snowy winter days. Miso, a staple of the Japanese kitchen, is extremely healing. Once cooked, the soup continues to thicken as it sits on the stove or in the refrigerator. Enjoy it as is, or thin it with extra miso broth.*

You can make this soup in advance, but for optimal taste it's best to add the miso at the last minute, either before you leave your house or when you arrive at your friend's house and are reheating the soup. ♥ SERVES 4 TO 6

1 ounce dried shiitake mushrooms

1 tablespoon olive oil

2 cups thinly sliced leeks, including light green parts, thoroughly rinsed

1 teaspoon minced garlic

1/2 teaspoon dried thyme or marjoram

1/2 cup dry white wine or vermouth

6 cups vegetable stock or broth (see Note)

3 large carrots, trimmed, peeled, halved lengthwise, and cut into 1/2-inch-thick slices

1/2 cup pearl barley, rinsed

1/2 cup hot water

3 to 4 tablespoons sweet white miso

Salt to taste

3 tablespoons minced fresh flat-leaf parsley, for garnish

1. Break off the shiitake stems, or pry them out with a sharp paring knife. Discard the stems or reserve them for stock. Break or chop the shiitake caps into tiny bits. Quickly rinse and drain. Set aside.

2. In a large, heavy soup pot, heat the oil over high heat. Sauté the leeks and garlic for 1 minute, stirring frequently. Add the thyme and wine and continue cooking over high heat until about half of the wine evaporates.

3. Add the vegetable stock, shiitakes, carrots, and barley, and bring to a boil. Reduce the heat to low, cover, and cook at a gentle boil until the barley is tender, 30 to 45 minutes.

4. Pour the hot water into a large glass measuring cup and dissolve 3 tablespoons of the miso in it by mashing the paste against the sides of the cup and stirring vigorously with a whisk or fork. Turn off the heat and stir the miso broth into the soup. Taste and add additional miso as needed for flavor, first dissolving the miso in a small amount of the soup's broth. Add salt, if needed.

5. Serve hot, garnished with the parsley.

NOTE: Make vegetable stock from scratch (page 22) or try a high-quality instant vegetable stock powder, such as Frontier brand (800-669-3275), available in many natural-food stores.

TO MAKE AHEAD: This soup is best eaten immediately after it is made, but you can prepare it through Step 3, let cool completely, cover, and refrigerate for up to 1 day. This soup does not freeze well.

TO REHEAT: Bring to a simmer over low heat and proceed from Step 4.

Cream of Leek and Potato Soup

In France, leek and potato soup is what a mother makes for her ailing child. Noted cooking teacher Mary S. Risley, owner of Tante Marie's Cooking School in San Francisco, created this easy, rustic soup that pairs mild leeks and blue cheese. If Stilton is unavailable, use another crumbly blue-veined cheese, such as Roquefort or Maytag Blue. If you or your friend does not like blue cheese, omit it and the soup will still be delicious. ♥ SERVES 4

1 tablespoon butter

1 shallot, finely chopped

2 leeks, including light green parts, well rinsed and coarsely chopped

2 cups chicken stock, preferably homemade (page 16), or low-sodium chicken broth

2 baking potatoes, peeled and cut into $^1/_2$-inch dice

$^1/_2$ to $^3/_4$ cup heavy cream

Coarse salt and freshly ground pepper to taste

Fresh lemon juice to taste

2 ounces Stilton cheese, crumbled

1. Heat the butter in a deep saucepan over medium heat; add the shallot and leeks and cook, stirring occasionally, until soft, about 10 minutes.

2. Add the stock and potatoes and simmer briskly until the potatoes are soft, about 20 minutes.

3. Puree using an emersion blender, or pass the soup through a food mill. Add the cream. Season with salt, pepper, and lemon juice and reheat over low heat for 2 or 3 minutes.

4. To serve, sprinkle each portion with Stilton.

TO MAKE AHEAD: Prepare through Step 3. Let cool completely, cover, and refrigerate for up to 5 days, or freeze in an airtight container for up to 3 months.

TO REHEAT: If frozen, let thaw in the refrigerator. Bring to a simmer over low heat. Proceed with Step 4.

Double Split Pea Soup

This soup by Lauren Groveman, from her book Lauren Groveman's Kitchen, *is substantial and richly flavored. The recipe yields enough for two meals, which allows you to make dinner for your own family and for another family you love. Or, you can easily halve the recipe. Lauren often leaves a batch in the refrigerator for people who might be exhausted after a long trip. "There's nothing better than coming home from the airport to a warm meal." This soup also freezes very well.* ❤ SERVES 14

7 quarts chicken stock (page 16) or low-sodium broth

2 pounds dried green split peas, rinsed and drained

1 pound dried yellow split peas, rinsed and drained

Meaty ham bone (shank) or 1 or 2 ham hocks, thoroughly scrubbed and rinsed

12 carrots, peeled

Salt to taste

4 tablespoons ($^1/_2$ stick) butter

2 large yellow onions, chopped

1$^1/_2$ cups trimmed, cleaned, and thinly sliced leeks

4 large garlic cloves, chopped

2 celery stalks, sliced

1$^1/_2$ teaspoons crumbled dried thyme

1 teaspoon crumbled dried oregano

Freshly ground pepper to taste

4 ounces smoked ham, diced (about 4 cups)

1 pound frozen peas, thawed

1. In a large heavy-bottomed stockpot, bring the stock or broth to a simmer. Stir in the green and yellow split peas and the ham bone or hocks. Bring back to a simmer, cover the pot, and cook over low heat for 1 hour.

2. Meanwhile, cut 8 of the carrots into irregular $^1/_3$-inch-thick slices and cut the remaining 4 carrots into diagonal slices. In a medium-sized saucepan, bring 2 quarts of water to a boil and place a large bowl of ice water on your counter. Add a little salt and the diagonally sliced carrots and boil until crisp-tender, 5 to 8 minutes. Drain and immediately plunge them into the bowl of ice water, swishing them around with your hand until cold. Drain the slices well and set aside.

3. Melt the butter in a large skillet over medium heat. Tear off a piece of waxed paper large enough to cover the interior of the skillet and brush some of the butter on one side. When the butter in the pan is bubbling, stir the onions, leeks, garlic, celery, and the 8 sliced carrots into the skillet, coating the vegetables well with butter. Add the thyme and oregano and place the buttered side of the waxed paper directly on top of the vegetables. Sweat the vegetables over very low heat, occasionally lifting the waxed paper to stir and redistribute them, for 15 to 20 minutes.

4. After the split peas have simmered for 1 hour, add the sweated vegetables to the stockpot and cover the pot securely. Simmer over low heat for 1 hour more. Remove from heat. Remove the ham bone or hocks from the pot and let cool to the touch.

5. Ladle the soup in batches into a large medium-mesh wire strainer set over a large bowl. As the strainer becomes full, transfer the solids to a blender or the bowl of a food processor fitted with the steel blade. Puree each batch of solids with a little of the stock until smooth, then transfer to another large bowl. You will end up with 1 large bowl of liquid and 1 large bowl of pureed vegetables.

6. Pour the vegetable puree into the empty stockpot and add enough stock to create the desired consistency. Remove any meat from the cooked ham bone or hocks and add to the soup; discard the bone. Add the salt, pepper, diced ham, thawed peas, and reserved blanched carrots to the soup. Cool uncovered to allow any grease to rise to the top; spoon off and discard the grease.

7. To serve, cover and reheat soup gently over low heat, stirring occasionally, until piping hot. Ladle into warmed, hefty wide soup mugs or deep bowls.

VARIATION: Although the flavor of this soup will be richest when using butter, you can reduce the overall amount of saturated fat in the recipe by omitting the butter and sweating the vegetables in ¼ cup extra-virgin olive oil and ¼ cup additional stock or broth. Alternatively, use half butter and half olive oil.

TO MAKE AHEAD: Let cool completely, cover, and refrigerate for up to 4 days, or freeze in airtight containers for up to 3 months. **TO REHEAT:** If frozen, let thaw in the refrigerator. Bring to a simmer over low heat.

White Bean Soup with Winter Greens

Adding a swirl of winter greens makes this healthful white bean soup from Fresh from the Farmers' Market *by Janet Fletcher almost a meal in itself. After the soup: a piece of cheese and some winter fruit, all highly portable accompaniments.* ♥ SERVES 6

1 pound dried cannellini or other white beans

¼ cup extra-virgin olive oil, plus more for garnish

1 large onion, chopped

2 carrots, cut into ⅓-inch dice

4 garlic cloves, minced

3 tablespoons minced fresh flat-leaf parsley

2 bay leaves

4 cups chicken stock (page 16) or low-sodium chicken broth

2 cups water

Salt and freshly ground black pepper to taste

¾ pound winter greens such as kale, chard, dandelion, collard, or turnip greens

Freshly grated Parmesan cheese

1. Rinse and pick over the beans. Soak them overnight in water to cover by 1 inch. Drain.

2. Heat the ¼ cup olive oil in a large pot over medium heat. Add the onion, carrots, garlic, parsley, and bay leaves. Sauté until the vegetables are slightly softened, about 10 minutes.

3. Add the drained beans, stock or broth, and water. Season with salt and pepper. Bring to a simmer, cover, and adjust heat to maintain a bare simmer. Cook, stirring occasionally, until the beans are tender, 45 minutes to 1½ hours. Remove the bay leaves. In a blender or food processor, puree 4 cups of the beans and vegetables with some of their liquid. Return to the pot and stir well. If needed, thin the soup with water.

4. Wash the greens well, removing any bruised leaves, thick ribs, or stems that are thick or tough. Stack the leaves a few at a time, roll into a log, and cut crosswise into ¼-inch-wide ribbons. Bring a large pot of salted water to a boil over high heat. Add the greens and boil until tender—a couple of minutes for young dandelion and turnip greens, longer for kale or collard greens. Drain, reserving about 2 cups of the cooking liquid. Stir the greens into the soup. Cover and simmer an additional 5 minutes. Thin the soup, if needed, with the reserved cooking liquid. Taste and adjust the seasoning.

5. Serve in warm bowls, topping each portion with a drizzle of olive oil and a sprinkle of cheese.

TO MAKE AHEAD: Prepare through Step 3. Let cool completely, cover, and refrigerate for up to 3 days. To freeze, prepare through Step 3 and store in an airtight container for up to 2 months.

TO REHEAT: Bring to a simmer over low heat. Proceed with Step 5. If frozen, thaw in the refrigerator, then bring to a simmer over low heat and proceed from Step 4.

Creamy Corn Soup

This creamy, yet creamless, soup appeared in Intimate Gatherings *by Ellen Rose and Jessica Strand. It is a wonderful combination of the comforting, sweet taste of corn and the spicy, tangy, peppery tastes of jalapeño and lime. If you want something more subtle and rich, you can omit the jalapeño, and add 1 cup of corn kernels sautéed in butter with a dollop of crème fraîche. If fresh corn isn't available, frozen corn will work in a pinch.* ♥ SERVES 4

2 tablespoons butter

2 leeks, white parts only, well rinsed and coarsely chopped

1 celery stalk, diced

1 small jalapeño, minced

4 cups corn kernels (about 8 ears corn)

3 cups strained vegetable broth (page 22), chicken stock
(page 16), or low-sodium chicken broth

Juice of 2 limes

2 cups milk

Salt and freshly ground pepper to taste

1/2 avocado, cut into thin slices, for garnish (optional)

Coarsely chopped fresh cilantro, for garnish (optional)

1. In a stockpot, melt the butter over medium heat. Add the leeks, celery, and jalapeño. Sauté until the leeks are translucent and the celery and jalapeños are soft. Add the corn and stir for 2 or 3 minutes. Add the broth or stock and the lime juice and simmer for 15 minutes.

2. In a blender or food processor, puree the soup in batches. For an extra smooth soup you can use a ricer.

3. Return the soup to the stockpot and slowly stir in the milk. Cook for 5 minutes, or until completely warm. Season with salt and pepper.

4. Serve hot, garnished with avocado slices and coriander, if you like.

NOTE: Because it's got such a creamy, smooth texture and subtle flavor, almost any garnish will complement this soup beautifully: chives, sour cream and salsa, dill, chopped tomatoes, chopped roasted red peppers, and even shredded smoked chicken with a dollop of guacamole.

TO MAKE AHEAD: Let cool completely, cover, and refrigerate for up to 1 week. Freeze in an airtight container for up to 1 month.

TO REHEAT: If frozen, let thaw at room temperature. Bring to a simmer over low heat.

Beef and Barley Soup with Mushrooms

Throughout its ten-thousand-year history, barley has played an important role in the kitchens of many cultures. For example, in the Middle East, the grain appears in belila, *a sweet, souplike syrup served to commemorate a baby's first tooth. This recipe from* A Good Day for Soup, *by Jeannette Ferrary and Louise Fiszer, calls for pearl barley, which means the grain has been hulled and polished. It is a rich, warming antidote to a cold winter day.* ♥ SERVES 10

2 tablespoons vegetable oil

2 pounds beef short ribs, excess fat removed

2 onions, chopped

2 carrots, diced

2 celery stalks, sliced

1 ounce dried porcini mushrooms, soaked in 1½ cups hot water
for 30 minutes

8 ounces button mushrooms, sliced

¼ cup tomato paste

3 cups beef stock or broth

3 cups water

2 cups pearl barley

¼ cup chopped fresh dill weed, or 1 tablespoon dried dill

Salt and freshly ground pepper to taste

1. In a large, heavy nonreactive pot, heat the oil over medium-high heat. Brown the short ribs on all sides. Remove and set aside. Add the onions, carrots, and celery to the pot and cook until lightly browned and soft, about 10 minutes. Strain the dried mushrooms, reserving the soaking liquid. Rinse to wash off sand, if any, and add to the pot with the fresh mushrooms. Cook for about 8 minutes. Stir in the tomato paste, stock or broth, water, and reserved soaking liquid. Bring to a boil and add the barley and short ribs. Reduce heat to a simmer, partially cover, and cook until the meat is tender, about 1 hour.

2. Remove the ribs from the soup, let cool to the touch, and cut the meat from the bones. Discard the bones and return the meat to the soup. Add the dill and cook for another 10 minutes. Season with salt and pepper.

TO MAKE AHEAD: Let cool completely, cover, and refrigerate for up to 2 days, or freeze in an airtight container for up to 1 month.

TO REHEAT: Bring to a simmer over low heat.

Curried Pumpkin Soup

Donata Maggipinto created this vibrantly colored, full-flavored soup for Halloween Treats. If you're serving the soup to children, you might want to leave out the curry and Tabasco. But even without the spicy accents, this soup is a winner—and it's healthful and quick to make, too. Be sure you use a good eating (sugar) pumpkin such as Jack Be Little, Munchkin, or Spookie, rather than a field pumpkin. Butternut squash is an able pinch hitter for any pumpkin, and if you are limited on time, canned pumpkin will do the trick. ♥ SERVES 6 TO 8

1 small sugar pumpkin, 4 to 5 pounds, or 2 cups canned pumpkin

2 tablespoons olive oil

1 tablespoon unsalted butter

1 onion, finely chopped

5 cups chicken stock (page 16) or low-sodium broth

1 baking potato, peeled and chopped

1 teaspoon canola oil

Salt to taste

2 teaspoons grated orange zest

1½ teaspoons curry powder

½ cup heavy cream (optional)

Dash of Tabasco sauce (optional)

Freshly ground pepper to taste

1. Cut the pumpkin in half through the center and scoop out the seeds and strings; reserve the seeds for roasting. Cut away the hard peel and chop the flesh. You should have about 6 cups.

2. In a large saucepan over medium-low heat, warm the olive oil with the butter. When the butter melts, add the onion and sauté, stirring occasionally, until translucent, 2 to 3 minutes. Add the stock or broth, pumpkin, and potato, raise the heat to high, and bring to a boil. Reduce the heat to low, cover, and simmer until the vegetables are tender, 20 to 25 minutes.

3. Meanwhile, roast the pumpkin seeds: Preheat the oven to 350°F. Clean any flesh or strands off the reserved pumpkin seeds. In a small sauté pan over medium-high heat, heat the canola oil and sauté the seeds until lightly browned. Transfer them to a baking sheet and sprinkle with salt. Bake until crisp, about 10 minutes. Remove from the oven and drain on paper towels.

4. Working in batches, transfer the vegetables with some of the liquid to a blender or food processor and puree until smooth. Return the puree to the saucepan and stir in the orange zest and curry powder. Place over low heat and stir in the cream and the Tabasco, if using. Season with salt and pepper.

5. Heat to serving temperature. Ladle the soup into warmed bowls and sprinkle with the pumpkin seeds.

TO MAKE AHEAD: Prepare through Step 4 except for adding the cream and Tobasco. Let the soup cool completely, cover, and refrigerate for up to 3 days, or freeze in an airtight container for up to 2 months. Store the pumpkin seeds in a covered container in the refrigerator for up to 3 weeks.

TO REHEAT: If frozen, let thaw in the refrigerator. Bring to a simmer over low heat. Stir in the cream and Tobasco and proceed with Step 5.

CHAPTER 2

Casseroles, Baked Pastas, and Potpies

Casseroles and potpies are ideal portable dishes to carry to a friend's house. These homey, baked one-dish meals are comfort food staples around the world. Tamale pie, shepherd's pie, and macaroni and cheese are just three of the recipes in this chapter that will warm the heart and sustain the body.

Casserole refers to both the food and the container in which it is served. The container may be made of glass (Pyrex), earthenware, or enamel-lined cast iron. Casserole dishes come in a variety of sizes and shapes, including deep-sided baking dishes and shallow gratin dishes.

Like soups, casseroles can be made ahead, frozen, and reheated. Baking and reheating times are approximate and will vary, depending on whether the casserole is at room temperature when it goes into the oven. You can assemble the casserole and let your friends bake it, or you can bake it, let it cool completely, cover it tightly, and store it in the refrigerator. Bring to room temperature, then reheat in a microwave or in a preheated 350°F oven until hot.

Baked Rigatoni with Four Cheeses

An American classic is updated by James McNair with great cheeses. Although this recipe doesn't freeze well, it will keep in the refrigerator for up to 3 days. It can be reheated in a microwave or a preheated 350°F oven until heated through; to keep cheese smooth, avoid overbaking. ❤ SERVES 4 TO 6

1 tablespoon salt, plus more to taste

1 pound dried pasta such as fusilli, penne, rigatoni, or ziti

6 tablespoons (³/₄ stick) unsalted butter

¹/₂ cup all-purpose flour, preferably unbleached

4 cups milk

2 cups evaporated milk

Freshly ground pepper to taste

Freshly grated nutmeg to taste

1¹/₂ cups *each* freshly shredded Gruyère cheese (about 5 ounces),
    freshly shredded Emmenthaler cheese (about 4¹/₂ ounces),
    freshly shredded sharp Cheddar cheese (about 5 ounces)

1 cup freshly grated Parmesan cheese (about 4 ounces),
    preferably Parmigiano-Reggiano

1. Stir the 1 tablespoon salt into a large pot of rapidly boiling water. Drop the pasta into the boiling water and cook, stirring frequently, until tender but still firm to the bite. Drain into a colander, rinse under cold running water, drain again, transfer to a large bowl, and set aside.

2. Preheat the oven to 350°F. Grease a 9-by-13-inch baking dish and set aside.

3. In a heavy saucepan, melt the butter over low heat. Whisk in the flour and cook, whisking or stirring almost constantly, until bubbly and fragrant, about 5 minutes; do not brown. Remove from heat.

4. Meanwhile, in a saucepan, combine the milk and evaporated milk and bring just to a boil over medium-high heat. Pour all at once into the butter and flour mixture and whisk until smooth. Season with salt,

pepper, and nutmeg. Place the pan over medium heat and cook, whisking or stirring constantly, until thickened, about 5 minutes. Pour over the cooked pasta and stir to thoroughly coat the pasta. Spread the pasta evenly in the prepared baking dish.

5. In a bowl, combine the four cheeses, then sprinkle evenly over the pasta. Lightly dust the top with grated nutmeg and bake until the cheese melts and the pasta is heated through, about 25 minutes.

6. Transfer the baking dish to the broiler and cook until the cheese is slightly golden, about 3 minutes.

TO MAKE AHEAD: Store, covered, in the refrigerator for up to 3 days.

TO REHEAT: Heat in a microwave or a preheated 350°F oven until heated through.

Chicken Potpies

These savory, handheld pies make any meal or snack a celebration, especially when you prepare them ahead and bring them along to bake at your friend's home. In this recipe from Valentine Treats, *by Sara Perry, the flakey pies are shaped into hearts perfect for popping into your mouth. For a vegetarian version, simply leave out the chicken and increase the potatoes, carrots, and peas, or add other diced vegetables to your liking.* ♥ MAKES 6 INDIVIDUAL PIES

Filling:

½ cup shredded hash brown potatoes (frozen or leftover)

½ cup (about ¼ pound) finely chopped uncooked boneless, skinless chicken breast

¼ cup grated carrot

¼ cup frozen petite green peas

¼ cup shredded Cheddar cheese

¼ teaspoon *each* onion powder and celery salt

¼ teaspoon garlic powder

¼ teaspoon salt

¼ teaspoon ground black pepper

Pastry:

2 cups all-purpose flour

1½ teaspoons salt

½ cup vegetable shortening, cut into pieces

½ cup ice water

½ cup (1 stick) melted butter for brushing

1. To make the filling: In a bowl, combine the potatoes, chicken, carrot, peas, and cheese. Sprinkle the onion powder, celery salt, garlic powder, salt, and pepper over the mixture and toss. Set aside.

2. Preheat the oven to 375°F. Set aside a 5-inch heart cookie cutter or muffin cutter and two greased or parchment-lined baking sheets.

3. To make the pastry: In a bowl, whisk together the flour and salt. Add the shortening and use a pastry blender, two knives, or your fingertips to combine the mixture until it resembles coarse crumbs. Slowly add the ice water, stirring until the dough holds together. Do not overmix.

4. With lightly floured hands, gather the dough into a ball. On a lightly floured surface, divide the dough in half and flatten each half into a disk. Leave one disk out and refrigerate the other, wrapped with waxed paper or plastic wrap.

5. On a lightly floured surface, use a floured rolling pin to roll out the dough ⅛ inch thick. Use a cookie cutter to cut out hearts, collecting the trimmings to roll again. Use a spatula to transfer the hearts to the baking sheet, leaving ½ inch between them. Repeat with the remaining dough disk until you have twelve heart cutouts. Spoon about 3 tablespoons filling on top of 6 of the hearts. Place the remaining hearts over the filling. Use a fork to crimp the edges and poke a set of holes on top.

6. Brush the tops with the melted butter. Bake until golden, 35 to 40 minutes. Transfer to a wire rack and let cool until the crust is just warm to the touch. (Otherwise, the filling can be too hot for children.) Serve warm or at room temperature.

TO MAKE AHEAD: Prepare through Step 5, wrap tightly in plastic, and refrigerate for up to 1 day before baking. Proceed with Step 6. After baking, wrap tightly in aluminum foil and refrigerate for up to 1 week. Freeze, tightly wrapped in aluminum foil, for up to 1 month.

TO REHEAT: Reheat in a preheated 350°F oven until hot and bubbly, about 20 minutes.

French Shepherd's Pie with Celery Root and Potato Topping

Shepherd's pie, a traditional English dish, is meat stew covered with a thick layer of mashed potatoes and then lightly browned in the oven. In this version from Potager *by Georgeanne Brennan, the topping is a combination of mashed potatoes and pungent celery root.*

    Celery root has a somewhat intimidating appearance, but once the whorled and callused skin is removed, the flesh can be cooked or eaten raw in any number of different ways. If you are a purist, you can omit the celery root and substitute an extra potato instead. ♥ SERVES 4 TO 6

4 tablespoons butter

1$\frac{1}{2}$ to 2 pounds boneless lamb stew meat,
    cut into 1-inch pieces

3 fresh bay leaves, or 1 dried bay leaf

1$\frac{1}{2}$ teaspoons salt

1$\frac{1}{2}$ teaspoons freshly ground pepper

1 tablespoon all-purpose flour

1 cup beef stock or broth

4 potatoes, peeled and quartered

1 large celery root, peeled and cut into 1-inch cubes
    (see Note)

$\frac{1}{4}$ cup milk

1 egg

1 teaspoon chopped fresh thyme

1. Melt 1 tablespoon of the butter in a large skillet over medium-high heat. Add the lamb and brown lightly on all sides, about 10 minutes. Add the bay leaves, sprinkle with 1 teaspoon *each* of the salt and pepper and all the flour, and continue to cook, stirring constantly. The flour will start to brown on the bottom of the pan, but don't let it burn. Let it become very dark brown, as it is the browning flour that will eventually give the stew its rich, dark color. This will take 6 to 8 minutes. Stirring the meat and scraping the bottom, add the stock or broth, a little at a time, until all the bits of browned flour are freed from the pan bottom and mixed into the liquid. Cover the pan, reduce the heat, and simmer until the lamb is very tender and separates with a fork, 1½ to 2 hours. The cooking time will very because the age of meat sold as lamb ranges considerably from very young to almost a yearling.

2. While the lamb is cooking, boil the potatoes in water to cover until tender, about 30 minutes. At the same time, in a separate pan, boil the celery root in water to cover until tender. The celery root will take a little less time to cook—only 15 to 20 minutes—than the potatoes.

3. Drain the potatoes, reserving ¼ cup of their cooking water, and place them in a bowl. Drain the celery root and set aside 1 cup of the cubes to add to the stew. Add the remaining cubes to the potatoes and mash them together. Add the reserved potato cooking water, the milk, 2 tablespoons of the butter, the egg, the remaining ½ teaspoon *each* salt and pepper, and the thyme. Whisk until well blended and fairly smooth.

4. Preheat the oven to 375°F. To assemble the pie, put the stew in an ovenproof casserole and stir in the reserved celery root cubes. Spoon the potato mixture evenly over the top to cover completely. Cut the remaining 1 tablespoon butter into bits and dot the potato topping with the bits.

5. Bake until the topping is lightly browned and the stew is bubbling, 15 to 20 minutes.

NOTE: Once it is exposed to the air, cut celery root discolors. If you are not going to use the celery root immediately, put the cubes into a bowl of cold water to cover and add ¼ cup vinegar or fresh lemon juice to prevent discoloration.

TO MAKE AHEAD: Let cool completely, cover, and refrigerate for up to 2 days. This dish does not freeze well.
TO REHEAT: Dot with 2 teaspoons of butter, cover with aluminum foil, and reheat in a preheated 350°F oven until heated through, 20 to 25 minutes.

Tamale Pie

Marion Cunningham, the modern-day Fannie Farmer, featured this impressive dish in The Supper Book. *The sausage and beef, flavored with onions, corn, celery, cumin, tomatoes, and green chiles, cook in a thick cornmeal crust.* ♥ SERVES 6

6 cups water

1½ cups yellow cornmeal

3 teaspoons salt

4 tablespoons butter, or more to taste

½ pound bulk sausage

2 tablespoons chili powder

¾ teaspoon ground cumin

1 garlic clove, minced

1 to 1½ cups finely chopped onions

1 small green bell pepper, seeded, deribbed, and chopped

1 cup finely chopped celery

1½ pounds ground beef

3 cups canned plum (Roma) tomatoes, or 4 cups
    peeled and seeded fresh tomatoes (see page 53)

2 cups fresh, frozen, or canned corn kernels

One 4-ounce can diced mild green chiles, drained

1 teaspoon minced jalapeño chile (optional)

1 cup pitted ripe olives

2 cups grated medium or sharp Cheddar cheese

1. Bring 4 cups of the water to a boil in a 3-quart kettle. Stir the cornmeal into the remaining 2 cups cold water, then stir this into the boiling water. Continue to stir while the water returns to a boil. Reduce the heat to low, add 1½ teaspoons of the salt and the butter, cover, and simmer for 30 to 40 minutes, stirring often.

2. Mash the sausage in a large skillet, and cook over medium heat until it begins to turn color. Add the chili powder and cumin and cook about 5 minutes. Add the garlic, onions, green pepper, celery, and the remaining salt. Stir and cook until the vegetables are tender.

3. Crumble the beef into the pan and cook until it loses its raw color. Add the tomatoes, corn, diced chiles, and jalapeño, if using. Simmer for 15 to 20 minutes.

4. Preheat the oven to 350°F. Grease a 10-by-14-by-2-inch baking pan. Spread two-thirds of the cornmeal mixture on the bottom and up the sides of the pan. Spoon in the filling and distribute the olives evenly over it. Top with the remaining cornmeal, then sprinkle with the cheese. Bake until golden brown, about 1 hour.

TO MAKE AHEAD: Assemble casserole up to 1 day in advance and keep, covered in the refrigerator.

TO REHEAT: Reheat in the microwave or bake in a preheated 350°F oven until heated through.

Italian Risotto Frittata

Cookbook author Lou Seibert Pappas included the recipe for this hearty frittata in Omlettes, Soufflés & Frittatas. *It is an easy-to-make dish to deliver for brunch, lunch, or dinner. It can be served hot, at room temperature, or cold and is a fine way to use leftover rice.* ♥ SERVES 3 TO 4

6 eggs

Salt and freshly ground pepper to taste

1 tablespoon minced fresh oregano or basil

2 tablespoons butter or olive oil

¾ cup cooked Arborio or long-grain rice

½ cup diced Fontina or Gruyère cheese

2 ounces prosciutto, cut into julienne

2 green onions, including tender green parts, chopped

Cherry tomatoes and fresh basil sprigs for garnish (optional)

1. Preheat the broiler. In a medium bowl, beat the eggs, salt, pepper, and oregano or basil just until blended. In a medium skillet, melt the butter or heat the oil over medium heat and pour in the eggs. Spoon the rice, cheese, prosciutto, and onions over the eggs and reduce the heat to low. Shake the pan, slip a thin spatula under the eggs just as soon as they begin to set, and tilt the pan to let the uncooked portion flow underneath.

2. When the eggs are set, place under the broiler to brown the top lightly. Slide the frittata onto a warm plate and cut into wedges. Serve garnished with cherry tomatoes and basil sprigs, if desired.

TO MAKE AHEAD: Once cooked, the fritatta will keep, tightly wrapped in plastic in the refrigerator, for up to 2 days.

TO REHEAT: Serve cold, at room temperature, or reheat in a preheated 350°F oven for 5 to 10 minutes.

Spinach and Mushroom Chilaquiles

In Nuevo Tex-Mex, *Robb Walsh and David Garrido provide a nontraditional way to make a traditional Mexican comfort dish typically served for breakfast or lunch. Instead of sautéing the ingredients, they are layered and baked like a lasagna. This dish is best eaten right after it's made and makes a great housewarming gift.* ❤ SERVES 4

¼ cup olive oil, or as needed

12 corn tortillas (a great way to use up stale or broken tortillas)

1 pound mushrooms, preferably portobellos or crimini, stemmed and sliced

4 cups spinach leaves, chopped

Salt to taste

2 cups cooked white beans or canned white beans, drained

8 ounces jack cheese, thinly sliced

Green Sauce (recipe follows), or other high quality prepared green salsa

1. Preheat the oven to 300°F. In a medium skillet, warm ¼ cup olive oil over low heat. Add the tortillas one at a time and cook for 15 seconds on each side. Transfer to paper towels to drain.

2. When all of the tortillas have been heated, there should be at least 2 tablespoons olive oil left in the skillet. If not, add oil as needed and place over medium heat. Add the mushrooms and cook, stirring for 7 to 10 minutes, or until any liquid they have released has evaporated. Add the spinach and cook for 2 minutes longer, or until wilted. Season with salt and set aside.

3. Butter a 9-by-12-inch baking dish. Place 4 tortillas in the dish, covering the bottom completely and overlapping as necessary. Cover with one third of the spinach-mushroom mixture and one third of the white beans. Top with one third of the cheese slices and then one third of the sauce. Repeat the layers twice, ending with the sauce.

4. Bake for 20 minutes, or until heated through. Serve hot directly from the dish.

TO MAKE AHEAD: This dish is best served the day it is made and will keep, tightly covered, in the refrigerator overnight.

GREEN SAUCE

A salsa verde is usually made with tomatillos, onions, and fresh chiles. This more elaborate and flavorful green sauce was invented by chef Bruce Auden, of Biga in San Antonio. A jar of this sauce makes a great gift. Your friends can use it to accompany enchiladas and other cooked dishes or as a snack with chips. ♥ MAKES 1½ TO 2 CUPS

1 tablespoon olive oil

3 cloves garlic, halved

2 serrano chiles, stemmed and minced

6 green onions, including tender green parts, chopped

6 tomatillos, husked and quartered

1 cup dry white wine

3 poblano chiles, stemmed, roasted, peeled, and seeded (see Note)

1 cup chopped fresh cilantro

Salt to taste

1. In a medium skillet, heat the olive oil over high heat. Add the garlic, serranos, green onions, and tomatillos and cook, stirring occasionally, for 4 to 6 minutes, or until the tomatillos start to discolor slightly. Deglaze with the wine, scraping the bottom of the pan to dissolve any browned bits, and bring to a boil. Boil for 30 seconds.

2. Transfer the contents of the skillet to a blender, add the poblano chiles and cilantro, and puree until smooth. Season with salt.

NOTE: To roast chiles pierce a pepper with a fork and hold over a gas flame, about 4 inches from the heat source. Keep turning the pepper until it is evenly charred on all sides. The pepper skins should turn black when properly roasted. Place the roasted peppers in a plastic bag and seal the bag. Allow the peppers to sweat in the bag for about 10 to 15 minutes. When you remove them from the bag they will be easy to peel. Rinse the peppers under cool running water. Remove and discard the skin. Cut in half and discard the seeds and veins.

TO MAKE AHEAD: The sauce will keep, tightly capped, in the refrigerator for up to 2 days.

Ready to Cook!
Polenta
Lasagn.
375-0

Polenta Lasagna with Tomatoes and Peppers

The first polenta lasagna Diane Rossen Worthington ever tasted was made with rich layers of the classic Bolognese and béchamel sauces alternating with the cornmeal filling. This variation takes into account the inherent heaviness of polenta and lightens up the lasagna with a fluffy spinach filling and a bold pepper-tomato sauce. You won't miss the noodles in this crowd pleaser, which is an ideal vegetarian one-dish meal from American Bistro. ♥ SERVES 6 TO 8

1 tablespoon olive oil

1 small onion, very finely chopped

1 garlic clove, minced

½ teaspoon salt

7 cups chicken stock (page 16) or low-sodium broth

2 cups instant polenta

7 tablespoons freshly grated Parmesan cheese

Two 10-ounce packages frozen chopped spinach, thawed

Two 15-ounce containers low-fat ricotta cheese

Salt and freshly ground pepper to taste

Pinch of freshly grated nutmeg

4 cups Red Pepper–Tomato Sauce (recipe follows)

2 cups shredded mozzarella cheese

1. Lightly coat a 9-by-13-inch baking dish with non-stick cooking spray or oil. In a large saucepan, warm the olive oil over medium heat. Add the onion and sauté for 3 to 5 minutes, or until softened. Add the garlic and sauté for 1 minute more, making sure it does not brown. Add the salt and stock or broth and bring to a rolling boil over medium heat.

2. In a thin stream (a measuring cup with a lip works well for pouring), very slowly add the polenta, stirring constantly with a wooden spoon. Reduce the heat to low and continue cooking for 3 to 5 minutes, stirring constantly to be sure it doesn't stick, until it is very thick, smooth, and creamy. Stir in 3 tablespoons of the Parmesan cheese.

3. Pour the polenta into the prepared baking dish, smoothing the top with a rubber spatula if necessary. Let the polenta rest for at least 2 hours to set.

4. Squeeze out all of the water from the spinach. In a small bowl, mix the spinach with the ricotta cheese. Season with salt, pepper, and nutmeg.

5. Preheat the oven to 375°F. Invert the polenta onto a cutting surface. Set the dish aside to use again. Cut the polenta rectangle in half crosswise to make 2 rectangles each measuring 9 by 6½ inches. (This will make it easier to transfer the polenta back into the baking dish later on.) Cut a 2-foot long piece of dental floss and hold

continued

it taut between your hands. Working with 1 piece of polenta at a time, place the floss against the end farthest from you and pull the floss toward you, through the center of the polenta piece, slicing it in half to give you a top and a bottom layer. (Alternatively, use a serrated knife to slice through the polenta.) Repeat with the second rectangle.

6. Spoon 1 cup of the Red Pepper–Tomato Sauce evenly on the bottom of the same baking dish. Put 2 of the polenta pieces in the dish to cover the bottom. Spoon half of the spinach-ricotta mixture over the polenta, using the back of a spoon to spread it out, then sprinkle with 1 cup of the mozzarella and 2 table-spoons of the Parmesan cheese. Spoon 2 cups of the sauce over the cheese.

7. Top with the remaining polenta pieces, covering the sauce completely. Spoon the remaining spinach-ricotta mixture evenly over the polenta. Sprinkle the remaining 1 cup mozzarella over the top. Dot with the remaining 1 cup sauce, leaving small gaps between the sauce. Sprinkle with the remaining 2 tablespoons Parmesan. (The lasagna will be high, slightly above the rim of the dish.)

8. Put the lasagna dish on a baking sheet to catch any drips. Bake, uncovered, for 30 minutes. Remove from the oven and let sit for 10 minutes. To serve, cut into serving portions and use a spoon or spatula to scoop them out onto individual dishes.

TO MAKE AHEAD: Prepare through Step 7, cover, and refrigerate for up to 1 day. Remove from the refrigerator 1 hour before baking and proceed with Step 8. Freeze in an airtight container for up to 1 month.

TO REHEAT: Bake in a preheated 350°F oven until heated through, 15 to 20 minutes.

RED PEPPER–TOMATO SAUCE

This sauce is easy to prepare, and a wonderful alternative to traditional tomato sauces. Here half of a chipotle chile has been added to deepen the flavor and add a hint of full-bodied heat. If you prefer a milder sauce, omit the chile. ♥ MAKES ABOUT 4 CUPS

3 tablespoons olive oil

1 onion, finely chopped

4 large red bell peppers, seeded and thinly sliced

2 large tomatoes, peeled, seeded, and finely chopped
   (see note)

½ canned *chipotle en adobo,* coarsely chopped

1 bunch fresh basil, coarsely chopped

Salt and freshly ground pepper to taste

1. In a large nonaluminum saucepan, heat the olive oil over medium heat. Add the onion and sauté for 3 to 5 minutes, or until softened.

2. Add the bell peppers, tomatoes, chile, and basil, cover partially, and cook over medium-low heat until the peppers are softened, about 20 minutes. Remove from the heat.

3. Puree the vegetables in a food processor fitted with the metal blade for about 1 minute, or until the mixture is smooth with some texture remaining. Add the salt and pepper. Taste for seasoning.

NOTE: To peel and seed tomatoes, cut an X in the blossom ends and drop into a pot of boiling water for 30 to 60 seconds, or until the skin starts to wrinkle. Using a slotted spoon, transfer quickly to a bowl of cold water to halt the cooking. When cool to the touch, remove the skins and cut in half crosswise. Hold each half upside down over the sink and shake and squeeze the tomato gently to release the seeds.

TO MAKE AHEAD: Let cool completely, cover, and refrigerate for up to 3 days, or freeze for up to 1 month.

TO REHEAT: If frozen, let thaw in the refrigerator. Bring to a simmer over low heat.

Baked Eggplant Parmesan
(Melanzana alla Parmigiana)

While eggplant parmesan is mostly known to Americans in its southern Italian mozarella-laden configuration, Joyce Goldstein presents this deliciously light version in Enoteca. *The eggplant takes on a meltingly tender quality upon reheating. This gratin can be assembled ahead of time and baked just before serving.* ♥ SERVES 6

3 globe eggplants, about ³/₄ pound each

Salt for sprinkling

Olive oil for frying

2 cups peeled, seeded, and diced tomatoes (see page 53)

2 garlic cloves, minced (optional)

Salt and freshly ground pepper to taste

³/₄ cup grated Parmesan cheese

1¹/₂ cups fine dried bread crumbs

1. Peel the eggplants and cut into crosswise slices about ¹/₃ inch thick. Put the slices in 1 or 2 colanders and sprinkle them with salt. Let drain for 30 minutes. Press gently with a kitchen towel or more paper towels to squeeze out the remaining moisture, then wipe away excess salt with paper towels. (Do not rinse; the eggplant will absorb water.)

2. Preheat the oven to 400°F. Oil a 9-by-12-inch baking dish.

3. Pour olive oil to a depth of ¼ inch into a large sauté pan, preferably nonstick, and place over medium-high heat. When the oil is hot, add the eggplant slices in batches and fry, turning once, until golden and tender. Transfer to paper towels to drain. Add oil to the pan only as necessary to prevent sticking, or the porous eggplant will drink more than it needs. The frying should take about 6 minutes for each batch.

4. Add the tomatoes to the pan and cook until they break down and acquire a saucelike consistency, about 10 minutes. Add the garlic, if using, during the last 2 minutes. Season with salt and pepper.

5. Spread a thin layer of the tomato sauce in the prepared baking dish. Add half of the eggplant slices, then half of the remaining tomato sauce. Top with the remaining eggplant and then the remaining sauce. Scatter the grated cheese and then the bread crumbs evenly over the surface.

6. Bake the eggplant until golden, about 25 minutes. Let rest for 15 minutes before serving.

TO MAKE AHEAD: Prepare through Step 5, cover, and refrigerate for up to 1 day before baking. Or, after baking, let cool completely, cover, and refrigerate for up to 3 days.

TO REHEAT: This dish is best reheated in a microwave, but can be reheated in a preheated 350°F oven until heated through.

Lasagna Casserole with Meat and Red Wine Sauce

The perfect portable dish, lasagne is the perenial favorite to bring from your house to theirs. This rustic meat lasagna appears in The Pasta Book *by Julia della Croce. The dish goes together easily and quickly and is as good for midweek meals as it is for entertaining.* ♥ SERVES 6

$1/2$ ounce dried porcini mushrooms

3 tablespoons olive oil

3 tablespoons unsalted butter

1 medium to large onion, finely chopped

1 large garlic clove, finely chopped

3 tablespoons chopped fresh flat-leaf parsley leaves

1 large carrot, peeled and finely chopped

1 large stalk celery, including leaves, finely chopped

$1/2$ pound lean, sweet, fennel-flavored Italian pork sausages
    (about 3 links)

1 pound lean ground beef or pork

4 tablespoons tomato paste

$3/4$ cup good dry red wine

One 28-ounce can tomatoes in puree, drained and
    coarsely chopped, puree reserved

$1^1/2$ teaspoons salt, or to taste, plus 2 tablespoons for
    cooking pasta

Freshly ground pepper to taste

2 tablespoons vegetable oil

1 pound dried lasagna or narrower lasagnette noodles

3 cups (24 ounces) ricotta cheese

Good pinch of freshly grated nutmeg

$1^1/2$ cups freshly grated Parmesean cheese

$1/2$ pound thinly sliced Italian salame such as soppressata, diced

$1^1/2$ pounds good-quality mozzarella cut into very thin slices,
    or shredded

1. Soak the dried mushrooms in ¼ cup warm water until softened, about 30 minutes. Strain the liquid through a fine sieve and reserve. Chop the mushrooms coarsely. Set aside.

2. Heat the olive oil and butter in a heavy saucepan. Add the onion, garlic, parsley, carrot, and celery. Sauté over medium heat until the vegetables are softened, about 10 minutes; do not let them brown. Remove the sausage meat from the casings. Add it and the ground meat to the pan. Sauté until lightly browned, about 8 minutes, breaking up the meat with a spoon and mixing it with the vegetables. Sauté gently another 8 to 10 minutes. Stir in the reserved mushrooms and their liquor, the tomato paste, and wine; simmer for 5 minutes. Add the tomatoes and their reserved puree; simmer gently, uncovered, until the sauce thickens, about 30 minutes. Season with salt and pepper.

3. Meanwhile, preheat the oven to 425°F. Place an oven rack in the upper half of the oven. Bring 5 to 6 quarts water to a rolling boil and add the 2 tablespoons salt, vegetable oil, and noodles. Stir immediately, continuing to stir frequently as the noodles cook. Drain when slightly underdone (they will continue to cook in the oven), reserving ⅓ cup of the cooking water. Immediately rinse the lasagne noodles well in cold water to prevent them from sticking together.

4. Combine the ricotta with the reserved pasta water, nutmeg, and ½ cup of the Parmesan cheese. Smear the bottom of a 10-by-14-inch baking pan with a little of the meat sauce. Then place a single solid layer of the noodles on top, without overlapping. Spread a layer of the ricotta mixture on the noodles, followed by a layer of sauce. Sprinkle with some of the salame, add a layer of mozzarella, then sprinkle with several teaspoons of the remaining Parmesan cheese. Repeat layering until all the ingredients are used up, ending with a layer of meat sauce strewn with mozzarella and Parmesan. Be sure to cover the pasta with sauce to prevent it from drying out in the oven.

5. Bake until the lasagne is heated through and bubbly, about 25 minutes. Remove from the oven and let settle for 10 to 15 minutes. Cut into squares before serving.

TO MAKE AHEAD: The lasagne can be assembled up to 4 days in advance. Once cooked, it will keep, covered, in the refrigerator for up to 5 days, or freeze for up to 6 months
TO REHEAT: If frozen, let thaw in the refrigerator. Reheat in a preheated 350°F oven until heated through.

Baked Conchiglione with Spinach-Ricotta Filling

This baked pasta from Pasta Harvest *by Janet Fletcher is a pretty sight with the rich tomato sauce bubbling around the plump shells, stuffed face up. It's best to assemble it at your house and then bake it at your destination, where you can bring it to the table and serve it directly from the baking dish. Janet always boils a few extra shells (more than the 20 required) to allow for breakage.* ♥ SERVES 4

½ pound spinach leaves, thick stems removed (from about
   ¾ pound untrimmed spinach)

2 garlic cloves, minced

1 cup whole-milk ricotta cheese

½ pound whole-milk mozzarella cheese, coarsely grated

1 egg, lightly beaten

1 tablespoon finely minced fresh basil

Salt and freshly ground pepper to taste

20 conchiglione (jumbo shells)

2 teaspoons olive oil

1½ cups homemade tomato sauce (page 71), or
   high-quality canned

½ cup freshly grated pecorino romano cheese

1. Preheat the oven to 375°F. Lightly oil a baking dish large enough to hold the shells in one layer.

2. Wash the spinach carefully in a sink filled with cold water. Transfer to a medium skillet with just the water clinging to the leaves. Cover and cook over medium heat until the leaves are just wilted, about 3 minutes, tossing once or twice with tongs so the leaves wilt evenly. Transfer the wilted leaves to a sieve and place under cold running water until cool. Drain well and squeeze dry. Chop finely.

3. In a medium bowl, combine the spinach, garlic, ricotta, mozzarella, egg, basil, salt, and pepper. Mix well.

4. Cook the shells in a large pot of boiling salted water until not quite al dente, about 8 minutes. Drain the shells and transfer them to a bowl. Toss with the olive oil to keep them from sticking together.

5. Put half the tomato sauce on the bottom of the prepared dish. Fill each shell with a heaping tablespoon of the stuffing. You should have just enough stuffing to fill the 20 shells. Arrange the shells in a single layer in the dish. Spoon the remaining sauce over and around the shells. Top with the pecorino cheese. Cover with aluminum foil and bake until bubbling hot, 30 to 40 minutes.

TO MAKE AHEAD: You can assemble this dish up to 1 day in advance and refrigerate. Bake the casserole at your destination. (This casserole doesn't hold very well after baking so eat up!)

Turkey Tetrazzini

Turkey tetrazzini is a nostalgic comfort food that is sure to bring back fond memories of mom's cooking. Diane Morgan's easy version from The Thanksgiving Table *will make a wonderful gift on a cold day.* ♥ SERVES 8

2$\frac{1}{2}$ teaspoons salt

12 ounces spaghetti

6 tablespoons unsalted butter

6 tablespoons all-purpose flour

3$\frac{1}{2}$ cups turkey stock or low-sodium chicken broth

$\frac{3}{4}$ cup heavy cream

2 teaspoons minced fresh rosemary

1 tablespoon fresh thyme

$\frac{1}{4}$ teaspoon freshly grated nutmeg

Freshly ground pepper to taste

3$\frac{1}{2}$ cups $\frac{1}{2}$-inch dice of roast turkey

10 ounces frozen green peas

$\frac{1}{2}$ cup dried bread crumbs

$\frac{1}{2}$ cup (2 ounces) grated Parmesan cheese

1. Fill a large stockpot three-fourths full of water, cover, and bring to a boil. Add 2 teaspoons of the salt and the spaghetti and cook until al dente (cooked through but still slightly chewy), 8 to 10 minutes. Drain, rinse under cold water, and set aside.

2. Preheat the oven to 375°F. Butter a 9-by-13-inch baking pan. In a medium sauté pan or skillet, melt the butter over a medium heat. Add the flour and cook, stirring, until faintly colored, about 2 minutes. Gradually whisk in the stock until the sauce is smooth and thickened, 3 to 5 minutes. Whisk in the cream, then add the remaining ½ teaspoon salt, the rosemary, thyme, nutmeg, and pepper. Stir in the turkey and peas and heat through. Taste and adjust the seasonings, then remove from the heat.

3. Put the pasta in the prepared dish and spoon the turkey mixture over it. In a small bowl, combine the bread crumbs and the Parmesan. Sprinkle evenly over the sauce. Bake, uncovered, until heated through and bubbly, about 20 minutes. Turn on the broiler and quickly brown the top of the casserole.

TO MAKE AHEAD: Let cool completely, cover, and refrigerate for up to 3 days, or freeze for up to 1 month.

TO REHEAT: If frozen, let thaw in the refrigerator. Reheat in a preheated 350°F oven until heated through.

Noodle Kugel

Many Jewish cooks treasure kugel recipes that have been handed down through the generations. There is the potato kugel and the noodle kugel, and each in turn has its own variations. Best of all, kids love kugel—especially noodle kugel. This sweet version by Joan Zoloth from Jewish Holiday Treats *is typical of the eastern European tradition. The yield is generous and the leftovers are delicious.* ♥ SERVES 10 TO 12

12 ounces flat wide egg noodles

$\frac{1}{2}$ cup (1 stick) margarine or butter, at room temperature

2 apples, peeled, cored, and diced

$\frac{1}{2}$ cup golden raisins, rinsed

4 eggs, beaten

Salt to taste

Cinnamon sugar for sprinkling

1. Preheat the oven to 375°F. Generously grease a 9-by-13-inch baking dish.

2. Bring a large saucepan of lightly salted water to boil, add the noodles, and boil until al dente, 5 to 10 minutes. Drain and place in a large bowl. Add the margarine or butter, apples, and raisins and mix well. Add the eggs, season with salt, and mix well. Spoon the mixture into the prepared baking dish. Sprinkle with cinnamon sugar.

3. Bake until the top is golden brown and crisp, 35 to 45 minutes. Remove from the oven and serve hot or cold, cut into squares.

TO MAKE AHEAD: Let cool completely, cover, and refrigerate for up to 3 days, or freeze for up to 1 month.

TO REHEAT: If frozen, let thaw in the refrigerator. Reheat in the microwave or in a preheated 350°F oven until heated through.

Potato and Portobello Mushroom Casserole

Here's a simple recipe from one of San Francisco's best French chefs, Hubert Keller of Fleur de Lys. If you want to add a little love, Keller says to add some shaved fresh black truffle to the mushrooms and sauté them together. This casserole is best eaten the day it is made. ❤ SERVES 4

3 pounds russet potatoes
½ cup finely chopped onion
3 tablespoons finely diced carrot
3 tablespoons finely diced celery
1 leek, white part only, well rinsed and julienned
4 garlic cloves, minced

3 tablespoons olive oil
2 portobello mushrooms, stems and gills removed, sliced
Salt and freshly ground pepper to taste
½ cup dry white wine
1½ cups vegetable stock (page 22) or broth

1. Preheat the oven to 400°F. Lightly oil a 6-by-9-by-2-inch earthenware or glass casserole dish.

2. Peel and wash the potatoes. Slice them into rounds about ⅛ inch thick. Toss the potatoes in a large mixing bowl with the onion, carrot, celery, leek, and garlic.

3. Heat the olive oil in a sauté pan over high heat. When the oil is very hot, add the mushrooms and toss constantly for 2 to 3 minutes, or until they are moist and tender. The heat should remain high but the mushrooms should not brown. Remove the mushrooms from the pan, season with salt and pepper, and set aside.

4. Arrange half of the potato mixture in the prepared dish. Season with salt and pepper. Layer half of the mushrooms over the potato mixture. Cover with the remaining potato mixture, season with salt and pepper, then top with the remaining mushrooms. Pour in the wine and broth. The liquid should come about halfway up the sides of the potatoes and mushrooms.

5. Seal the casserole very tightly with 2 or 3 layers of aluminum foil, making sure that no steam can escape during baking.

6. Bake for about 1¼ hours, or until the potatoes are tender and can be cut easily with a fork.

TO MAKE AHEAD: Let cool completely, cover, and refrigerate overnight.
TO REHEAT: Reheat in the microwave or in a preheated 350°F oven until heated through.

Macaroni and Cheese

In Saveur Cooks Authentic American, *this dish was featured as classic American comfort food. Good cheddar, Wisconsin or otherwise, makes all the difference.* ❤ SERVES 6

1 pound short macaroni

Salt to taste

8 tablespoons butter

6 tablespoons all-purpose flour

$^1/_2$ teaspoon cayenne

Freshly ground white pepper to taste

$3^3/_4$ cups hot milk

4 cups grated Cheddar cheese

$^1/_2$ cup heavy cream

$^1/_2$ cup fresh bread crumbs

1. Preheat the oven to 350°F. In a large pot of boiling, salted water, cook the macaroni until al dente, about 10 minutes. Drain thoroughly.

2. Meanwhile, melt 6 tablespoons of the butter in a heavy, medium saucepan over medium-low heat. Add the flour and cook, stirring constantly, for about 4 minutes. (The flour mixture must foam as it cooks, or the sauce will have a raw-flour taste.) Stir in the cayenne and salt and white pepper to taste. Whisk in the hot milk, about a cup at a time, and cook, whisking constantly, until the sauce thickens. Reduce heat to low and stir in 2 cups of the cheese. Cook, stirring, until the cheese melts, about 2 minutes.

3. Combine the cheese sauce and drained macaroni in a large bowl and season with salt, if needed. Sprinkle $^1/_2$ cup cheese over the bottom of a buttered 8-by-11-inch baking dish. Put one-third of the pasta in the dish, top with another $^1/_2$ cup of the cheese, then repeat the layering twice, ending with cheese.

4. Pour cream over the assembled macaroni and cheese. Melt the remaining 2 tablespoons butter over medium heat. Add the bread crumbs and stir to coat well with the melted butter, then sprinkle over the macaroni and cheese. Bake until golden, about 30 minutes. Allow to rest for 15 minutes before serving.

TO MAKE AHEAD: Let cool completely, cover, and refrigerate for up to 3 days. Freeze in an airtight container for up to 1 month.
TO REHEAT: If frozen, do not thaw. Reheat in microwave or in a preheated 350°F oven until warm.

CHAPTER 3

Roasts, Braises, and Stews

Roasts, braises, and stews are great gifts for anyone who needs to have hearty food on hand. Although they can take a few hours to cook, they often call for few ingredients and require little effort or attention. Best of all, they make great leftovers for other meals or to use in other recipes. Leftover roast chicken, for example, can go into a variety of casseroles.

Most braises and stews can be made ahead of time and kept covered in the refrigerator for 3 or 4 days, improving in flavor when left to sit for a day before serving. Roasts are typically best served warm from the oven, but many will keep, tightly wrapped, in the refrigerator for up to 4 days. This chapter is primarily for meat eaters, but a few fish dishes and recipes for vegetarians are included.

Slowly cooked and rich with flavor, roasts, braises, and stews remind us to spend time with people we love.

Roast Chicken with Lemon, Garlic, and Rosemary

Roast chicken—perhaps second only to chicken soup—is the quintessential comfort food. In Cooking for the Week, *Diane Morgan, Kathleen Taggart, and Dan Taggart recommend cooking two birds for guaranteed leftovers—great for making casseroles, potpies, and other weekday dinners. When bringing this meal to a friend, pack up both chickens along with a recipe for the leftovers, or make the leftovers dish yourself and deliver it on a second visit.* ❤ SERVES 4 TO 6 WITH LEFTOVERS

2 whole fresh chickens ($4\frac{1}{2}$ to $4\frac{3}{4}$ pounds each)

$\frac{1}{2}$ cup (1 stick) unsalted butter

Juice of 2 lemons (quarter and reserve squeezed lemons)

4 garlic cloves, halved lengthwise

Salt and freshly ground pepper to taste

6 sprigs fresh rosemary, each about 3 inches long

1. Preheat the oven to 375°F. Remove the sacks of giblets from the chickens. Freeze the neck, heart, and gizzards for stock, and fry the liver for a four-legged friend. Pull out and discard any large fat deposits from the cavities of the chicken. Trim any loose skin and trim off the tails. Pat dry with paper towels.

2. Line a large roasting pan with aluminum foil for easy cleanup, unless the pan is nonstick. Put a roasting rack or large wire cake rack in the pan. In a small saucepan, melt the butter over low heat. Add the lemon juice, garlic, salt, and pepper. Heat through.

3. Set the chickens on the roasting rack, breast-side up. Put 3 rosemary sprigs and 4 lemon quarters in each cavity. Brush the seasoned butter on the birds, coating them well. Put the roasting pan in the lower half of the oven and roast, basting every 20 minutes, until the juices run clear when a sharp knife is inserted into the thickest part of the thigh, or when an instant-read thermometer registers 170°F inserted at the same point, about 1 hour.

4. Remove the chickens from the oven, baste again, and cover loosely with aluminum foil. Leave 1 chicken to cool completely. Let the other chicken rest for 10 minutes, then carve and serve. To save leftovers, cut the other chicken in half, wrap each half well, and store in the refrigerator for up to 4 days.

VARIATION: Cut peeled root vegetables such as potatoes, carrots, leeks, onions, sweet potatoes, turnips, and parsnips into 1-inch chunks. Coat with olive oil or melted butter, sprinkle with salt and pepper, and place in the roasting pan to roast with the chicken.

TO MAKE AHEAD: Let the chickens cool completely, wrap well, and refrigerate for up to 4 days.

Chicken Simmered with Tomatoes, Fresh Herbs, and Red Wine

Hunter's style chicken, popularly known as chicken cacciatore, is cooked in varying ways throughout Italy. This is Ayla Algar's delicious version. ❤ SERVES 4

3 tablespoons olive oil

1 chicken (about 3 pounds), legs and thighs halved and breast quartered

1 small onion, chopped

1 garlic clove, minced

¼ cup dry red wine

2 cups chopped tomatoes

1 cup sliced mushrooms

1 or 2 green bell peppers, seeded, deribbed, and sliced

1 teaspoon chopped fresh thyme

1 teaspoon chopped fresh marjoram

Salt and freshly ground pepper to taste

1. Heat the olive oil in a large skillet over medium heat. Add the chicken, onion, and garlic and sauté until the chicken is golden brown. Pour in the wine and simmer, uncovered, for about 10 minutes.

2. Stir in the tomatoes, mushrooms, green peppers, herbs, salt, and pepper. Cover and simmer about 20 minutes, or until the chicken is tender.

TO MAKE AHEAD: Let cool completely, cover, and refrigerate for up to 3 days.

TO REHEAT: Bring to a simmer over low heat.

Classic Burgundy Beef

The Burgundy region has a tradition of amplitude in cooking, a kind of old-fashioned grandmotherly largesse that suffuses its cuisine, and this rich beef braise by Brian St. Pierre, from The Perfect Match, *is the best example of it: a comforting signature dish. If your friends are up for a glass of wine, the perfect match is also red burgundy, of course.* ♥ SERVES 6

1 large onion, chopped

2 carrots, peeled and chopped

2 thyme sprigs

2 bay leaves

3 cups dry red wine

3 tablespoons olive oil

2 pounds beef chuck roast, cut into 1½-inch cubes

5 bacon slices, chopped

16 small (boiling) onions, peeled

2 tablespoons flour

2 garlic cloves, chopped

1 cup beef broth

8 ounces button mushrooms

Salt and freshly ground pepper to taste

2 tablespoons chopped fresh flat-leaf parsley

Boiled potatoes for serving

1. In a glass bowl, combine the onion, carrots, herbs, wine, and 2 tablespoons of the olive oil. Add the beef, cover, and refrigerate for at least 6 hours or overnight. Remove the meat from the marinade and pat dry with paper towels. Strain the marinade, discard the vegetables, and reserve the liquid.

2. In a large, heavy casserole or Dutch oven, heat the remaining 1 tablespoon olive oil over medium heat. Add the bacon and whole onions and sauté for about 5 minutes, or until lightly browned. Using a slotted spoon, transfer to a dish. Increase the heat to medium-high and brown the meat in batches on all sides. Using a slotted spoon, transfer to a dish.

3. Add the flour to the hot fat and stir vigorously. Return the beef to the pan and add the marinade, stirring well. Bring to a brisk simmer and add the garlic and broth. When the liquid bubbles, reduce heat to a low simmer, cover, and cook for 2 hours. Add the bacon, onions, mushrooms, salt, and pepper. Cook for another 30 minutes. Serve garnished with the parsley and accompanied with the boiled potatoes.

TO MAKE AHEAD: Let cool completely, cover, and refrigerate for up to 5 days. Freeze in an airtight container for up to 2 months.

TO REHEAT: If frozen, thaw in the microwave or in the refrigerator. Reheat in a microwave or in a preheated 350°F oven until heated through.

Beef Chili

Known by the Spanish chili con carne, one of America's most popular dishes started out as a campfire stew for hungry Texas cowboys. Today there are nearly as many "authentic" recipes for chili as there are cooks in the Lone Star state, some swearing by cubed beef instead of ground and most arguing against the beans that are added in other parts of the country.

This easy, yet tasty, version comes from James McNair's sister, Martha, who serves it with a choice of condiments and warm tortillas for wrapping the chili to eat out of hand. This dish is especially good to bring to families with children who appreciate a hearty meal. ❤ SERVES 6 TO 8

3 pounds round or other tender boneless lean beef, trimmed of excess fat and connective tissue

3 tablespoons canola or other high-quality vegetable oil

2 cups finely chopped white or yellow onion

1 tablespoon minced garlic

¾ cup ground dried ancho, pasilla, or other mild to medium-hot chile

1 tablespoon ground cumin, or to taste

½ cup all-purpose flour

Salt, freshly ground black pepper, and ground cayenne to taste

3 cups Tomato Sauce (recipe follows) or high-quality commercial tomato sauce

4 cups cooked dried or canned black or pinto beans (optional)

Condiments:
Freshly shredded Cheddar cheese
Sour cream
Finely chopped red onion
Chopped fresh tomato
Fresh cilantro (coriander) leaves

1. Quickly rinse the beef under cold running water and pat dry with paper toweling. Using a sharp knife, cut the beef into ½-inch cubes, or chop finely with the knife or in a food processor. Set aside.

2. In a heavy stew pot over medium heat, heat the oil. Add the onion and cook until tender but not browned, about 5 minutes. Add the beef and garlic and cook, breaking up the meat with a spoon, until the beef is just past the pink stage. Add the chile, cumin, flour, salt, pepper, and cayenne. Stir in the tomato sauce, adjust the heat to maintain a simmer, and cook, uncovered, until thickened and the flavors are well blended, about 1 hour.

3. Drain the beans, if using, and stir them into the chili during the last 20 minutes of cooking. Add a little water to the pot any time during the cooking if the mixture begins to dry out.

4. To serve, place the condiments in small bowls on the table. Ladle the chili into warmed bowls and serve hot.

TO MAKE AHEAD: This chili is best eaten within 2 days, but will keep in an airtight container in the refrigerator for up to 2 days. Freeze in airtight containers for up to 1 month.

TO REHEAT: If frozen, let thaw in the refrigerator. Bring to a simmer over low heat.

TOMATO SAUCE

During tomato season, make several batches of this sauce and freeze for winter use. Whenever flavorful summer tomatoes are unavailable, canned tomatoes make a much better sauce than hothouse supermarket varieties. If you like, add minced fresh or crumbled dried herbs or minced fresh or crushed dried hot chile to taste.

This sauce can also be tossed with pasta, stirred into risotto, added to soups, or served over meat, poultry, or fish. ❤ MAKES ABOUT 4 CUPS

½ cup extra-virgin olive oil, or ½ cup (1 stick) unsalted butter

1 cup finely chopped yellow onion

1 cup finely chopped carrot

1 cup finely chopped celery or fennel

2 teaspoons minced garlic, or to taste

4 cups peeled, seeded, drained, and chopped ripe (see page 53) or canned tomatoes

1 teaspoon sugar, or to taste

Salt to taste

1. In a saucepan, heat the oil or butter over medium-high heat. Add the onion, carrot, and celery or fennel and cook, stirring frequently, until soft and lightly golden, about 5 minutes. Add the garlic and cook for 1 minute longer. Stir in the tomatoes, sugar, and salt. Reduce the heat to low and simmer, uncovered, until thick, about 30 minutes. For a smoother sauce, transfer to a food processor or blender and puree.

TO MAKE AHEAD: Let cool completely, cover, and refrigerate for up to 5 days, or freeze for up to 1 month.

TO REHEAT: If frozen, let thaw in the refrigerator. Bring to a simmer over low heat.

Ratatouille

Many experts on the cuisine of Nice, where this dish originated, suggest that you cook the vegetables individually and marry them together. However, the editors at Saveur magazine found that sautéing ratatouille vegetables separately and then cooking them together yields superior results. Make more ratatouille than you need so there'll be some to eat later, hot or cold. ♥ SERVES 8

3 globe eggplants, cut into 2-inch cubes

4 zucchini, quartered lengthwise and cut into 2-inch pieces

2 tablespoons kosher salt, plus more to taste

½ cup extra-virgin olive oil

6 yellow onions, peeled and thinly sliced

4 green or red bell peppers, cored, seeded, and
   cut into 1-by-2-inch strips

6 small tomatoes, peeled, seeded (see page 53),
   and quartered

8 garlic cloves, minced

20 fresh basil leaves

1 bunch fresh flat-leaf parsley, stems trimmed

8 fresh thyme sprigs

Freshly ground pepper to taste

1. Put the eggplant and zucchini in 2 separate colanders and toss each with 1 tablespoon salt. Let drain for 30 minutes. Blot dry with paper towels. (Do not rinse; the vegetables will absorb water.)

2. Heat 2 tablespoons of the oil over medium-low heat in a large skillet. Add the onions and sauté until translucent, about 15 minutes, then transfer to a bowl and set aside. Add 2 tablespoons of the oil to the same skillet and increase heat to medium-high Add the eggplant and sauté until golden, about 20 minutes. Transfer the eggplant to a large heavy pot with a cover and spoon a thin layer of onions on top. Add 2 tablespoons of the oil to the skillet, then add the zucchini and sauté until golden, about 10 minutes. Transfer to the pot and cover with a thin layer of onions. Add 1 tablespoon of the oil to the skillet, then add peppers and sauté until edges turn

brown, about 15 minutes. Transfer to the pot and cover with a thin layer of onions.

3. Add the remaining 1 tablespoon oil to the skillet and add the tomatoes, garlic, and basil, lightly crushing the tomatoes with the back of a fork. Cook until slightly thickened, about 15 minutes. Transfer to the pot and add the remaining onions, parsley, thyme, salt, and pepper.

4. Simmer, partially covered, over low heat, gently stirring occasionally, for 1½ hours. Adjust seasoning, then cook about 30 minutes more.

TO MAKE AHEAD: Let cool completely, cover, and refrigerate for up to 3 days.

TO REHEAT: Reheat in a microwave or bring to a simmer over low heat until heated through.

Tagine of Lamb with Prunes

This classic tagine recipe, from Cooking at the Kasbah *by Kitty Morse, combines sweet and savory flavors. The word* tagine *refers to the glazed earthenware vessel with a conical lid in which this Moroccan dish is traditionally cooked. Kitty recommends cooking this stew in a heavy Dutch oven, reheating it at your destination, and serving it in a traditional tagine pot, if possible, for an authentic presentation.* ♥ SERVES 4

2 tablespoons olive oil

1 teaspoon ground turmeric

1 teaspoon ground ginger

1³⁄₄ pounds lamb sholder, or ³⁄₄ pound leg of lamb trimmed of fat and cut into 2-inch cubes

2 onions, 1 finely diced, 1 finely sliced

1 cup low-sodium chicken broth

8 threads Spanish saffron, toasted and crushed (see Note)

15 fresh cilantro sprigs, tied with cotton string

1 cup pitted prunes

2 tablespoons honey

1 teaspoon ground cinnamon

¹⁄₂ teaspoon fresh ground pepper

Salt to taste

1 tablespoon unhulled sesame seeds, toasted (see page 95)

Crusty bread for serving

1. In a small Dutch oven or enameled casserole over medium-high heat, heat the olive oil and sauté the turmeric, ginger, and lamb until the meat is well coated and lightly browned, 2 to 3 minutes. Add the diced onion to the meat along with the broth, saffron, and cilantro. Cover and reduce the heat to medium-low. Cook until the meat is fork tender, 1 to 1½ hours.

2. Preheat the oven to 200°F. With a slotted spoon, transfer the meat to an ovenproof dish and keep warm in the oven until ready to serve. Discard the cilantro. Bring the sauce in the casserole back to a simmer.

3. Add the sliced onion, prunes, honey, cinnamon, and pepper to the simmering sauce. Season with salt. Cook until the mixture thickens somewhat, 6 to 8 minutes.

Spoon the sauce over the meat and sprinkle the dish with the sesame seeds. Serve with warm bread.

NOTE: Toasting saffron before use releases the precious spice's essential oils. Put the threads in a small nonstick skillet and stir constantly over medium-high heat until fragrant, 2 or 3 minutes. Transfer immediately to a bowl and stir to stop the cooking. Crush the threads between your fingers, or pound them in a mortar with a pinch of salt before using.

TO MAKE AHEAD: Let cool completely, cover, and keep in the refrigerator for up to 2 days. Freeze in airtight containers for up to 2 months.

TO REHEAT: If frozen, do not thaw. Reheat in a preheated 350°F oven until heated through.

Little Meat Loaves

According to Bob Sloan, author of The Working Stiff Cookbook, *a plate of meatloaf and mashed potatoes, will make you a kid again. If you are a working stiff, this is an excellent dish to make on a weeknight for friends who have children. You can substitute ground turkey for the ground beef or use a mixture of the two meats. Leftover meatloaf makes great sandwiches for a late-night snack or lunch the next day.* ♥ SERVES 4

2 slices bread, crusts trimmed, cut into $^1/_2$-inch cubes

$^1/_2$ cup milk

1 pound lean ground sirloin or ground round

2 eggs, lightly beaten

1 small onion, grated

$^1/_4$ cup barbecue sauce

1 tablespoon chili powder

1 teaspoon garlic powder or chopped fresh garlic

1 teaspoon Worcestershire sauce

$^1/_2$ teaspoon dried oregano

Dash of Tabasco sauce (optional)

1. Preheat the oven to 375°F. Place an oven rack in the center of the oven.

2. Put the bread cubes in a medium mixing bowl. Add the milk and stir to coat all of the bread. Add the remaining ingredients and mix well, using your hands. Shape the mixture into 4 oval loaves about 7 inches long and 3½ inches wide at the center. Place the loaves in an ungreased 9-by-13-inch baking dish so they aren't touching.

3. Bake for 35 to 40 minutes, or until cooked through. Remove from the oven and let cool for about 3 minutes before serving.

VARIATION: To make a traditional-sized meatloaf, increase the ground meat to 1½ pounds. (You could add another half-pound of ground beef, veal, turkey, or pork.) Mix everything together and place in lightly greased loaf pan. Bake for 50 minutes on the center rack of a pre-heated 375°F oven. Let cool 5 minutes before slicing.

TO MAKE AHEAD: The meat loaves may be prepared through Step 2 the night before, covered with plastic wrap, and refrigerated. (The loaves may need slight adjusting to restore their shape before baking.) Once baked, let cool completely, cover, and refrigerate for up to 3 days, or wrap tightly in foil and freeze for up to 1 month.

TO REHEAT: Cover in foil (to keep in the juices) and heat in a preheated 350°F oven until heated through, about 20 minutes. If frozen, heat wrapped in foil, in a preheated oven until warm, 30 to 40 minutes. You could also slice them and reheat the slices in a microwave—1 minute, turn over, and cook 45 seconds more.

Mom's Meatball-Stuffed Peppers

Michael Chiarello, host of the public television series Michael Chiarello's Napa, *cookbook author, and founder of Napa Style, in Saint Helena, California, credits his favorite meatball recipe to his mother. Here, her meat mixture is stuffed into peppers for a dish that travels easily to a friend's house.* ♥ SERVES 4

6 large yellow bell peppers

1 pound ground sirloin

1 large egg

2 tablespoons freshly grated Parmesan cheese

2 tablespoons finely chopped fresh flat-leaf parsley

1 teaspoon dried oregano

2 tablespoons finely chopped fresh basil

1 cup finely chopped onion

1 cup fine dried bread crumbs or Progresso plain or seasoned
  bread crumbs

1 tablespoon sea salt (preferably gray), plus more to taste

1/2 teaspoon freshly ground pepper, plus more to taste

1 1/2 cups water

2 cups Quick Tomato Sauce (recipe follows),
  or high-quality tomato sauce

2 tablespoons Gremolata (recipe follows)

1. Preheat the oven to 350°F. Bring a pot of water to a boil and add salt. Cut off the lids of the peppers and reserve. Seed and derib the peppers, leaving them whole. Cut a small slice from the bottom of each pepper so it will stand upright. Add the peppers and lids to the pot of boiling water and cook until softened, about 10 minutes. Drain and let cool.

2. In a large bowl, mix together the meat, egg, cheese, parsley, oregano, basil, onion, bread crumbs, the 1 tablespoon salt, the 1/2 teaspoon pepper, and 1 cup of the water. Knead the water into the meat mixture with your hands. Add another 1/2 cup water and knead again. By now the mixture should feel smooth, with no grittiness left, and have a very soft texture.

3. Sprinkle the insides of the peppers with salt and pepper. Spoon a little tomato sauce into the bottom of each pepper and divide the meat mixture among them. Put upright in a flameproof baking dish and pour the remaining tomato sauce over and around the peppers. Top each pepper with its lid. Cover the dish tightly with a lid or aluminum foil lined with waxed paper or parchment paper. Bake until the peppers are soft and the filling has cooked through, about 1 hour.

4. Uncover the dish, remove the pepper lids, and dust the top of each pepper with about 1 teaspoon gremolata. Turn the oven to broil and place the peppers under the broiler just until browned, about 1 minute. Replace the lids and serve hot, warm, or at room temperature.

continued

TO MAKE AHEAD: Let cool completely, cover, and refrigerate for up to 2 days, or freeze for up to 1 month.

TO REHEAT: If frozen, thaw in the refrigerator. Reheat in a preheated 350°F oven until heated through.

QUICK TOMATO SAUCE

This is an all-purpose, fresh-tasting sauce (yes, even though made with canned tomatoes) for saucing pasta, spaghetti squash, or gnocchi; for serving with chicken; or for cooking fish fillets. If you can or have a large freezer, make big batches to keep on hand. Add a jalapeño chile to your sauce, if you wish. Left whole, it adds very little to no spiciness. ♥ MAKES ABOUT 3½ CUPS

One 28-ounce can whole tomatoes, preferably Muir Glen or S&W

3 tablespoons extra-virgin olive oil

½ cup finely chopped onion

1 tablespoon minced garlic

1 bay leaf

Salt and freshly ground pepper to taste

¼ cup drained oil-packed sun-dried tomatoes, chopped

1 tablespoon finely chopped fresh oregano

1. Pour off the tomato juice from the can into a bowl. Press the lid against the tomatoes to extract as much juice as possible. Then use your hand to squeeze the tomatoes to a pulp. Reserve the juice and pulp separately and set the empty can aside.

2. Heat the olive oil in a large, heavy saucepan over medium-high heat until hot. Add the onion to the pan and cook, stirring occasionally, until soft, about 2 minutes. Add the garlic and cook briefly until light gold. Add the tomato juice and bring to a boil. Simmer rapidly for several minutes. Add the crushed tomato pulp. Rinse the remaining pulp out of the can by filling it halfway with water and add that to the pan. Add the bay leaf, and salt and pepper and return to a boil. Add the sun-dried tomatoes and stir. Reduce heat to medium and simmer, stirring occasionally to prevent scorching, until the mixture thickens and the tomatoes have turned an orange-red versus the pale blue-red they were straight from the can, about 30 minutes. Add the oregano halfway through the cooking. Discard the bay leaf.

VARIATION FOR SUMMER TOMATO SAUCE: Substitute 2 pounds vine-ripened tomatoes for the canned tomatoes. Peel and seed the tomatoes (see page 53). Chop the tomatoes. Proceed as directed, omitting the sun-dried tomatoes and using jalapeño, if desired. You should have about 2¼ cups sauce. The recipe may be increased proportionately.

GREMOLATA

Gremolata is typically made with lemon zest, but this simple version may come in handy in so many ways: as a soup garnish, to pat on fresh sardines or other fish before roasting, or to sprinkle on vegetables, gratins, even toasted cheese sandwiches. To make a great, really simple pasta, just sauté a little garlic in olive oil until brown and toss with cooked pasta, gremolata, salt, pepper, and a spoonful of pasta cooking water. ♥ MAKES ABOUT ¼ CUP

1 tablespoon finely chopped pine nuts or hazelnuts, toasted (see page 93)

1½ tablespoons fine dried bread crumbs or Progresso plain or seasoned bread crumbs

1½ tablespoon finely chopped fresh flat-leaf parsley

⅛ teaspoon salt

Small pinch freshly ground pepper

1. Mix all the ingredients together in a small bowl. Refrigerate in an airtight container. Use within 3 days.

Basque-Style Fisherman's Stew

Loretta Keller, chef-owner of Bizou in San Francisco, likes to prepare this rustic stew on winter nights. Brimming with soul-satisfying flavors, it's so good your friends will find it hard to stop eating. Hearty country-style bread is the only accompaniment you'll need. ♥ SERVES 6

½ cup extra-virgin olive oil

2 onions, finely diced

3 russet potatoes, peeled and cut into 2-inch cubes

2 green bell peppers, seeded, deribbed, and chopped into 1-inch dice

2 garlic cloves, minced

Salt to taste

8 cups fish stock or bottled clam juice

1 cup dry white wine

6 ounces fresh tomatoes, peeled (see page 53), seeded, and diced, or ¾ cup diced canned tomatoes

2 pounds fatty fresh tuna (preferably from the belly), cut into large pieces

Freshly ground pepper to taste

Chopped fresh flat-leaf parsley for garnish

1. Heat the olive oil in a large, heavy saucepan over medium heat. Add the onions. Cover and cook, stirring occasionally, for about 10 minutes, or until the onions are translucent but not colored.

2. Add the potatoes, bell peppers, and garlic. Cook, stirring occasionally, for 10 minutes. Season lightly with salt.

3. Add the fish stock or clam juice and wine. Simmer for about 10 minutes, or until the potatoes are tender and the stew has thickened slightly.

4. Add the tomatoes and simmer for 10 minutes.

5. Add the tuna. Cover, remove from heat, and let stand until tuna is cooked until tender. Season with salt and pepper.

6. Ladle into bowls, garnish with parsley, and serve.

TO MAKE AHEAD: Prepare through Step 4 and refrigerate for up to 2 days.

TO REHEAT: Bring to a simmer over low heat. Proceed from Step 5.

Curried Tofu with Spinach and Tomatoes

This meatless meal by Lorna Sass from The New Soy Cookbook *is a welcoming dish with its curry-yellow tofu, bright green splashes of spinach, and cheery strips of tomato. Lorna particularly likes making this curry with frozen tofu, which thirstily drinks up the sauce and has a delightfully chewy texture. You'll also have good results with pressed fresh tofu.*

You can transport this curry in a colorful pot or in containers with tight-fitting lids. Serve the curry in shallow bowls over steamed basmati rice, with your favorite sweet mango chutney on the side. ♥ SERVES 3

1-pound block extra-firm or firm tofu, frozen, defrosted, and drained

1 tablespoon peanut oil or clarified butter

1 cup coarsely chopped onions

1 cup water, plus ¼ cup if necessary

¼ cup Patak's mild curry paste

3 tablespoons unsweetened grated dried coconut

3 large plum (Roma) tomatoes, cored and cut into eighths

¾ pound spinach, trimmed, rinsed, and coarsely chopped

Salt to taste

⅓ to ½ cup chopped fresh cilantro for garnish (optional)

1. Put the block of defrosted tofu between 2 plates and, pressing the plates firmly together, tip them over the sink as the tofu releases excess water. Release the pressure, then press the plates firmly together again 4 or 5 more times, or until no more water is expressed. With a serrated knife, slice the tofu into 1-inch cubes. Set aside.

2. Heat the oil in a large, heavy saucepan or wok over medium-high heat. Sauté the onions, stirring frequently, until lightly browned, about 3 minutes. Add the water and blend in the curry paste and coconut. Stir in the reserved tofu, taking care to coat it thoroughly with the curry sauce. Stir in the tomatoes.

3. Cover and cook over medium heat, stirring occasionally, until the tomatoes are soft, about 5 minutes. If the mixture seems quite dry, stir in the additional ¼ cup water at this point. Add the spinach. (If your pot isn't big enough, you may need to add half, cover, and let it wilt before adding the remainder.) Cover and continue cooking until the spinach is tender, 2 to 3 minutes. Season with salt.

4. Serve garnished with the cilantro, if you like.

TO MAKE AHEAD: Let cool completely, cover, and refrigerate for up to 3 days.

TO REHEAT: Bring to a simmer over low heat. Stir in a bit more water if needed.

CHAPTER 4

Salads and Sides

When a whole meal might be too much food for a friend to eat, a simple salad or warm vegetable dish might be just the thing he or she needs.

These nutritious salads and sides can be eaten as meals in themselves or as an accompaniment to other recipes in this book. You can bring the warm vegetable dishes straight from the oven or assemble them ahead of time and bake them at your destination. Most of the salads can also be assembled ahead of time and kept at room temperature for up to 2 hours or covered and refrigerated for as long as overnight.

Tailgate Potato Salad

When Barbara Lauterbach's daughter Lisa had her first child, Barbara loaded her car with enough food to sustain the new family over that first anxious week. This salad, from Barbara's book Potato Salad, *was among the offerings; the sweet potatoes and butternut squash provided nutrition for the new mother, while the tangy dressing and tart cranberries were refreshing.*

♥ SERVES 6 TO 8

1/2 pound small sweet potatoes

1 1/2 pounds Yukon Gold potatoes

1/2 pound butternut squash, peeled and cut into 1/4-inch cubes

Dressing:

1/2 cup sugar

1 teaspoon dry mustard

1/2 teaspoon salt

2 tablespoons grated yellow onion

1/3 cup cider vinegar

1 cup canola oil

1 tablespoon celery seed

1/4 cup chopped fresh curly parsley

1/4 cup dried cranberries

1/4 cup chopped red onion

1/4 cup chopped walnuts, toasted

1. Preheat the oven to 400°F. Scrub the sweet potatoes with a stiff brush but do not peel. Prick in several places with the tines of a fork. Bake until just tender when pierced with a fork, about 30 minutes. Alternatively, scrub and prick the potatoes and microwave on high for 6 to 8 minutes. Don't overcook or they won't cut nicely. Let cool completely and cut into 1/4-inch cubes.

2. In a large pot filled with water, boil the Yukon Gold potatoes for 20 to 25 minutes, or until just tender. Drain well. When cool, peel and cut into 1/4-inch cubes.

3. Cook the butternut squash cubes in boiling water to cover until just tender, about 5 minutes. Drain well.

4. While the potatoes are cooking, make the dressing: In a bowl, mix together the sugar, dry mustard, and salt. Stir in the onion and 2 tablespoons of the cider vinegar and mix until smooth. Gradually beat in the oil and the remaining vinegar. Add the celery seed. Blend well.

5. To assemble the salad, in a large bowl, gently mix together the Yukon Gold potatoes, sweet potatoes, squash, and parsley. Add the dried cranberries, red onion, and walnuts, then pour the dressing over all. Mix gently. Cover and refrigerate, then bring to room temperature before serving.

TO MAKE AHEAD: The dressing can be made up to 2 days ahead, covered, and refrigerated. Once dressed the salad will last, covered in the refrigerator, for up to 2 days.

Bradley Ogden's Mashed Red Potatoes

The beauty of this recipe by San Francisco chef Bradley Ogden is that you don't have to peel the potatoes. The skin stays on to add flavor and color. The recipe calls for garlic, but you can omit this ingredient if you don't happen to be a garlic lover. Just before serving, you can also stir in snipped chives and crème fraîche. These mashed potatoes are best served right after they are made.

♥ SERVES 6

$1^{1}/_{2}$ pounds small red potatoes

1 head fresh garlic

1 cup cream or half-and-half

1 cup milk, or more to taste

$^{1}/_{4}$ cup unsalted butter ($^{1}/_{2}$ stick)

Kosher salt and freshly ground pepper to taste

1. Preheat the oven to 350°F. Cook the potatoes in salted water until tender. Drain the potatoes and dry them out in the oven for 10 minutes.

2. While the potatoes are cooking, peel all the cloves from the head of garlic and, in a small saucepan, simmer them with the cream or half-and-half, milk, and butter. When the garlic is very tender, set the mixture aside.

3. Puree the potatoes and the garlic mixture through the medium disk of a food mill. Season to taste with salt and pepper. If necessary, thin with more milk. Keep warm until serving.

Green Bean Salad with Yellow Pepper, Jicama, and Tomato

Full of crunchy, sweet vegetables, this salad from A Taste of Summer *by Diane Rossen Worthington travels very well and makes a cheery, healthful addition to any occasion.* ♥ SERVES 4 TO 6

Salad:

1 pound green beans

1 yellow sweet pepper, seeded and julienned

1 medium jicama (about $\frac{1}{2}$ pound), peeled and julienned

15 cherry tomatoes, halved

Dressing:

1 teaspoon Dijon mustard

$\frac{1}{3}$ cup fresh lemon juice

1 teaspoon finely chopped fresh chives

$\frac{2}{3}$ cup olive oil

Salt and freshly ground pepper

1. To make the salad. Bring a medium saucepan of water to a boil. Immerse the green beans and cook for 7 to 10 minutes, depending on their size. The beans should be slightly crisp. Drain and plunge immediately into ice water to stop the cooking. When cool, drain well and place in a medium bowl.

2. Add the peppers, jicama, and tomatoes to the green beans. Toss gently to blend.

3. To make the dressing, in a small bowl, combine the mustard, lemon juice, and chives. Whisk to combine, then slowly add the olive oil, whisking until totally emulsified. Season with salt and pepper.

4. Drizzle the dressing over the vegetables and toss thoroughly. Taste for seasoning. Transfer to a serving bowl, cover, and refrigerate until well chilled, at least one hour.

TO MAKE AHEAD: Prepare up to 8 hours in advance and refrigerate until serving.

Caramelized Roasted Vegetables

Peggy Knickerbocker includes this hearty vegetarian main course in her book, Olive Oil. *You can integrate whatever catches your eye at the market. If peppers are out of season, omit them. If they are readily available, use more, perhaps even a combination of red, orange, and yellow. This is a free-form, rustic dish.* ❤ SERVES 6 TO 8

1 sweet potato, peeled and cut into $^1/_2$-inch-thick slices

1 unpeeled russet potato, cut into $^1/_2$-inch-thick slices

2 green zucchini, cut into $^3/_4$-inch-thick slices

2 yellow zucchini or summer squash, cut into
$^3/_4$-inch-thick slices

1 eggplant, cubed, salted, allowed to drain for 30 minutes
in a colander, and patted dry

1 head garlic, broken into unpeeled cloves

2 yellow onions, cut into 9 wedges each

1 fennel bulb, trimmed and sliced into wedges

1 or more red bell peppers, seeded and cut lengthwise into
$^1/_2$-inch-wide strips

$^1/_2$ cup extra-virgin olive oil

Salt and freshly ground pepper to taste

2 fresh rosemary sprigs, or 1 tablespoon dried rosemary

1. Preheat the oven to 400°F. Arrange all the vegetables in 3 or more large roasting pans, drizzle with the olive oil, and sprinkle with salt and pepper. Using your hands, toss the vegetables so that all of them are evenly coated. Break up 1 of the rosemary sprigs and distribute it over the vegetables, or sprinkle the dried rosemary over them.

2. Roast until the vegetables are brown and tender, turning them once or twice to avoid sticking, about 1 hour. Transfer to a large platter and serve warm, with a sprig of rosemary on top.

TO MAKE AHEAD: Let cool completely and store at room temperature for up to 4 hours, or covered in the refrigerator for up to 3 days. Bring to room temperature before reheating.
TO REHEAT: Reheat in a preheated 350°F oven for 10 to 15 minutes.

Braised Lentils with Bacon

Basque chef Gerald Hirigoyen, co-owner of San Francisco's much-acclaimed Fringale and Pastis restaurants, created this recipe with only five ingredients—not counting salt, pepper, and water. Lentils are quick to make and very nutritious. ❤ SERVES 4

$\frac{1}{4}$ **pound sliced bacon, cut crosswise into** $\frac{1}{2}$**-inch pieces**

$\frac{1}{4}$ **cup olive oil**

$\frac{1}{2}$ **large onion, coarsely chopped**

$\frac{2}{3}$ **cup dried lentils**

3 cups water

$\frac{1}{2}$ **teaspoon salt**

Freshly ground pepper to taste

5 tablespoons butter

1. Put the bacon into a saucepan and add water to cover. Bring to a simmer, then remove from heat and drain in a sieve. Rinse the bacon and drain again.

2. Put the bacon in a large saucepan with the olive oil and onion. Sauté over medium-high heat until the onion has softened, about 3 minutes. Add the lentils, water, salt, and pepper. Simmer, uncovered, until the lentils are tender and moist but not all of the liquid has evaporated, approximately 30 minutes.

3. Just before serving, add the butter and heat over low heat, stirring, until it melts. Taste and adjust the seasoning.

TO MAKE AHEAD: Let cool, cover, and refrigerate for up to 3 days.

TO REHEAT: Bring to a simmer over a low heat.

Autumn Rice with Red Peppers and Pine Nuts

This rice dish by Diane Rossen Worthington, from her book The Cuisine of California, *is decorated with colorful red bell peppers, celery, parsley, and toasted pine nuts. The peppers are somewhat sweet, while the other ingredients maintain their distinctive flavors. Put this in a clear glass bowl for a lovely presentation.* ♥ SERVES 8

2 cups chicken stock (page 16) or low-sodium broth

1 cup long-grain white rice

$^1/_2$ teaspoon salt

$^1/_8$ teaspoon finely ground pepper

2 tablespoons unsalted butter

2 tablespoons oil

1 onion, finely chopped

$^1/_2$ cup $^1/_2$-inch-dice red bell pepper

$^1/_2$ cup $^1/_4$-inch-dice celery

3 tablespoons pine nuts, toasted (see Notes)

2 tablespoons finely chopped fresh flat-leaf parsley

1. In a medium saucepan, bring the chicken stock or broth to a boil over high heat. Stir in the rice, salt, and pepper. Reduce heat to low, cover, and simmer for 20 minutes, or until the rice has absorbed all the liquid and is tender. Remove from heat.

2. Meanwhile, in a medium skillet, melt the butter with the oil over medium heat. Add the onion and sauté, stirring occasionally, until soft. Add the red pepper and celery and continue sautéing for about 5 minutes. The vegetables should be cooked but slightly crisp.

3. When the rice is cooked, add the vegetables, pine nuts, and parsley. Toss with a fork, and taste for seasoning.

NOTES: Walnuts, pecans, or almonds may be substituted for pine nuts. To toast nuts, preheat the oven to 350°F. Spread the nuts on a sided baking sheet and toast, stirring once or twice, until fragrant and lightly browned, about 5 minutes for pine nuts, 3 to 5 minutes for slivered almonds, 8 to 10 minutes for walnuts (halved), pecans, and hazelnuts.

To skin toasted hazelnuts, wrap the nuts in a clean dishtowel ands rub them together until the skins are loosened. Transfer to a colander and shake off the loose skins.

TO MAKE AHEAD: Prepare up to 2 hours ahead without the pine nuts and keep at room temperature. For longer storage, let cool completely, cover, and refrigerate for up to 2 days.
TO REHEAT: Reheat in a double boiler until warm. Add the pine nuts before serving.

Soba Noodle Salad with Tamari Dressing

Quick-cooking soba noodles are highlighted in this popular pasta salad by Jeff Morgan of Dean & DeLuca from Dean & DeLuca: The Food and Wine Cookbook. *Salty, nutty tamari, tangy citrus, earthy shiitake mushrooms, and crunchy sesame seeds all combine to stimulate the senses in this refreshing combination. Note that there is a pronounced difference between clear, light, cold-pressed sesame oil and dark Asian sesame oil made from toasted seeds. Asian sesame oil is copper colored and more assertive on the palate, with a nutty flavor that gives these noodles their Asian flair. The chile sesame oil, which adds just a touch of heat, can be found in Asian markets and most supermarkets.* ♥ SERVES 4

Tamari Dressing:

$^1\!/_4$ cup tamari sauce

2 tablespoons fish sauce

3 tablespoons Asian (toasted) sesame oil

1 tablespoon chile sesame oil

2 garlic cloves, minced

1 teaspoon grated fresh ginger, or $^1\!/_2$ teaspoon ground ginger

Juice of 1 lime

1 tablespoon fresh orange juice

3 tablespoons sake (optional)

1 pound dried soba noodles

3 tablespoons peanut or canola oil

8 ounces shiitake mushrooms, stemmed and thinly sliced

Salt and freshly ground pepper to taste

1 tablespoon sake (optional)

3 oranges, peeled and segmented (see Notes)

1 cucumber, peeled, seeded, and cut into matchsticks

$^1\!/_4$ cup chopped fresh cilantro

$^1\!/_4$ cup sesame seeds, toasted (see Notes)

1 bunch green onions, including tender green parts, cut into 2-inch-long diagonal pieces

1. To make the dressing: In a large bowl, combine all the dressing ingredients and stir to blend. Let sit for 30 minutes.

2. In a large pot of boiling water, cook the noodles until tender, about 4 minutes. Drain. Rinse in cold water and drain well. Toss with 2 tablespoons of the dressing.

3. In a medium skillet, heat the oil over medium heat and sauté the mushrooms until browned. Salt and pepper lightly and stir in the sake, if using. Remove from heat and let cool.

4. Add the noodles to the bowl with the dressing. Toss to coat evenly. Add the oranges, cucumber, cilantro, and half the sesame seeds. Toss again. Transfer to a large shallow bowl. Scatter the mushrooms and green onions over the top, and then sprinkle with the remaining sesame seeds.

NOTES: To peel and segment citrus fruit, with a paring knife, cut off the external skin and any white pith from the fruit. Then slice each segment free from the connecting membrane. Discard membrane.

Toast sesame seeds in a dry sauté pan over medium heat, stirring constantly, until fragrant, 2 or 3 minutes.

TO MAKE AHEAD: Prepare up to 4 hours ahead and keep at room temperature, or let cool completely, cover, and refrigerate for up to 2 days.

Warm Moroccan Beet Salad with Tangerines

Chef Jody Denton's warm beet salad from The Secrets of Success Cookbook *is spiced with cinnamon, allspice, and cloves and bathed in a sauce of tangerine, lime, honey, and mint. The use of sweet spices with the earthy beets sets up a dramatic and delicious contrast, while the presence of tangerine juice, and zest provides a welcome dose of vitamin C. The bright colors of this dish will brighten any friend's day.* ❤ SERVES 4 TO 6

3 or 4 bunches baby beets, such as red, golden, candy stripe,
   or Chiogga, greens still attached

3 tablespoons extra-virgin olive oil

Salt and freshly ground pepper to taste

3 tablespoons water

$\frac{1}{8}$ teaspoon ground cinnamon

2 allspice berries, crushed

1 whole clove, crushed

2 tablespoons dried currants

1 tablespoon honey

1 tablespoon grated or finely minced tangerine zest

$\frac{1}{4}$ cup tangerine juice

$\frac{1}{2}$ cup tangerine segments (see page 94)

1 tablespoon chopped fresh mint

2 teaspoons fresh lime juice

1. Preheat the oven to 350°F. Remove the green beet tops. Trim and discard the woody stems. Rinse the remaining greens thoroughly and reserve. Rinse the beets thoroughly.

2. Put the beets in a large baking dish. Toss the beets with 1 tablespoon of the olive oil. Season with salt and pepper. Add the water to the dish. Cover with aluminum foil and roast until the beets feel tender when poked with a small knife or wooden skewer, about 45 minutes. Remove from the oven. When cool, peel the beets by rubbing them between your fingers or with a kitchen towel. Set aside.

3. Heat the remaining 2 tablespoons oil in a large sauté pan over medium heat. Add the roasted beets, cinnamon,

allspice, and clove. Gently toss the beets with the spices until fragrant, about 1 minute. Add the currants, honey, and tangerine zest and increase heat to high. Toss until the honey just begins to caramelize, being careful not to let it burn, about 1 or 2 minutes.

4. Add the tangerine juice and boil until the liquid is reduced to a thick syrup. Mix in the reserved beet tops and stir until wilted, about 30 seconds. Transfer the mixture to a serving bowl. Add the tangerine segments, mint, and lime juice. Season with salt and pepper. Serve warm.

TO MAKE AHEAD: Prepare up to 2 hours ahead and keep at room temperature, or let cool completely, cover, and refrigerate overnight. Bring to room temperature to serve.

Couscous Salad

Couscous, the favorite grain of North Africa, is really a pasta. This dish, which appears in Sam Gugino's Low-Fat Cooking to Beat the Clock, *goes together quickly. It's crisp and refreshing and surprisingly filling. Several brands of instant couscous are on the market. Check the directions in the recipe and on the box you buy to make sure they both use the same amount of water.*

♥ SERVES 4

1$\frac{3}{4}$ cups water

$\frac{1}{2}$ teaspoon salt, plus more to taste

1$\frac{1}{3}$ cups instant couscous

5 green onions

1 cup packed fresh mint leaves

1 pound Kirby (small pickling) cucumbers or other cucumbers

Two 15-ounce cans chickpeas

1 pound ripe tomatoes

$\frac{1}{2}$ cup roasted red peppers or pimentos from a jar

$\frac{1}{3}$ cup capers, drained

1 to 1$\frac{1}{2}$ lemons

2 tablespoons extra-virgin olive oil

2 teaspoons hot paprika, or 1$\frac{3}{4}$ teaspoons sweet paprika and $\frac{1}{4}$ teaspoon cayenne pepper

2 teaspoons ground cumin

Freshly ground black pepper to taste

1. Put the water in a 2-quart saucepan over high heat. Add the ½ teaspoon salt, cover, and bring to a boil. (Or put the couscous, the ½ teaspoon salt, and the water in a microwave-safe container. Cover and cook on high power for 6 minutes.)

2. Meanwhile, trim the bulb ends of the green onions, cut in thirds crosswise, and put into a food processor with the mint leaves. Pulse until coarsely chopped. (Or chop by hand.) Transfer to a large mixing bowl. Trim the ends of the cucumbers but do not peel (unless you are using cucumbers with waxy skin). Quarter the cucumbers lengthwise, then cut crosswise into ¼-inch-wide pieces. Add to the mixing bowl.

3. When the water in the saucepan comes to a boil, add the couscous, stir, and turn off the heat. Cover and let the couscous steam for 7 minutes. (If using a microwave, also let the couscous steam for 7 minutes.)

4. While the couscous steams, open the cans of chickpeas into a colander. Rinse briefly and let drain. Core the tomatoes and squeeze out the juice. Quarter the tomatoes and add to the food processor. Pulse until coarsely chopped. Add to the mixing bowl. Put the peppers in the food processor and pulse until coarsely chopped. (The vegetables may be chopped by hand.) Add to the mixing bowl along with the capers. Pat any moisture from the chickpeas with paper towels and add to the mixing bowl. Mix the vegetables well, but gently.

5. Juice 1 lemon into a small bowl and mix in the olive oil, paprika, cumin, salt, and pepper. Fluff the couscous with a large fork. Add to the mixing bowl with the vegetables. Add the dressing and mix well. Taste and add more salt and the juice from the remaining lemon half, if desired.

TO MAKE AHEAD: Let cool completely, cover, and refrigerate for up to 2 days.

CHAPTER 5

Sweets

They may not be at the top of the list of healthful foods, but sweets can satisfy us in times of need like nothing else. A plate of oatmeal cookies, a silky pudding, or a fruit dessert may be just what your friend requires to lift his or her spirits. Chocolate, of course, is a classic favorite, which is all the more reason to make chocolate pots de crème, chocolate bread pudding, brownies, or chocolate chip cookies in a get-better present.

Most of the sweets in this chapter can be transported on covered dishes. Carry bars and tarts on a pretty plate, and bring cookies in a decorated tin or in a cookie jar. Wrap sturdier baked desserts in a beautiful napkin or cloth, with a flower slipped into the knot. You can put the angel food cake (and other iced cakes) on a circle of cardboard slightly larger then the cake and transport it (carefully) in a cardboard box.

Butterscotch Pudding

This classic comfort-food pudding, from Diner Desserts *by Tish Boyle, is true-blue butterscotch—miles above the boxed-mix variety, but not much harder to make. Tish first made this pudding for her husband when he was recovering from surgery. Bring a batch to a friend who's under the weather or feeling down—it will immediately improve anyone's outlook. Bring along a separate container of freshly whipped cream for an indulgent accompaniment.* ❤ SERVES 6

$^{1}/_{3}$ cup cornstarch

$^{1}/_{2}$ cup firmly packed light brown sugar

$^{1}/_{2}$ cup firmly packed dark brown sugar

$^{1}/_{2}$ teaspoon salt

2 cups whole milk

1 cup half-and-half

3 large egg yolks

3 tablespoons unsalted butter, cut into tablespoons

2 teaspoons vanilla extract

1. In a medium saucepan, stir together the cornstarch, sugars, and salt. Gradually whisk in the milk and half-and-half. Place over medium-high heat and bring to a boil, whisking constantly. Remove from heat.

2. In a medium bowl, whisk the egg yolks until smooth. Whisk about 1 cup of the hot milk mixture into the yolks. Return to the saucepan and cook over medium heat, whisking constantly, until the mixture comes to a gentle boil. Continue to boil, whisking constantly, for 1 minute. Immediately remove the pan from the heat and whisk in the butter pieces until they are completely melted. Whisk in the vanilla. Cover the pudding with waxed paper and let cool to room temperature.

3. Spoon the pudding into a serving dish or individual containers, cover with plastic wrap (pressing it directly onto the surface of the pudding to prevent a skin from forming), and refrigerate for about 2 hours, or until well chilled.

TO MAKE AHEAD: Refrigerate, tightly covered, for up to 3 days.

Erna's Make-in-Your-Sleep Raspberry Rice Pudding

Rick Rodgers says he likes to whip up a batch of this rice pudding from his book On Rice *and share it with a sick friend while sitting on the edge of the bed. Rick's friend Erna Zahn is a born cook. This is how she makes her rice pudding, which she swears is so easy she can make it in her sleep. Erna's family likes rice cooked until it's soft, so she is able to skip the recooking step. But if you like your rice cooked firm, recook the leftover rice until it is soft before making the pudding.* ♥ SERVES 4 TO 6

1½ cups cooked rice, preferably medium-grain

1½ cups heavy cream

¼ cup sugar

¾ teaspoon vanilla extract

⅓ cup seedless raspberry preserves, stirred to loosen

½ pint fresh raspberries

1. In a medium saucepan, bring ¼ cup water to a simmer over low heat. Add the cooked rice and cover. Simmer until the rice is very soft, about 10 minutes. Drain, if necessary, and cool completely.

2. In a chilled medium bowl, using a hand-held electric mixer set at high speed, beat the cream, sugar, and vanilla until stiff.

3. Add the rice and raspberry preserves to the bowl and fold until combined. Cover and chill for at least 1 hour.

4. Spoon into dessert bowls and sprinkle with the raspberries.

TO MAKE AHEAD: This pudding is best eaten right after it is made but will keep, covered without the berries, in the refrigerator overnight.

Zuni Café's Chocolate Pots de Crème

This rich dessert has been served at Zuni restaurant since the early 1980s. Chef Judy Rodgers considers it the perfect indulgence for anyone who loves chocolate. This sweet is best eaten the day it is made. ♥ SERVES 6

6 ounces bittersweet chocolate, chopped

1½ cups heavy cream

1½ cups milk

¼ cup sugar

8 egg yolks

1. Preheat the oven to 300°F. Melt the chocolate with ½ cup of the cream in a 2-quart saucepan over low heat or in a bowl set over a pan of simmering water. Remove from heat.

2. Combine the remaining 1 cup cream, the milk, and sugar in a saucepan and warm over medium-low heat until the sugar dissolves.

3. Whisk the egg yolks in a medium bowl, then slowly stir in the warm cream mixture. Pour the resulting custard mixture through a fine sieve into the melted chocolate and stir to combine.

4. Divide the mixture among 6 custard cups and place them at least 1 inch apart in a baking pan. Add enough hot water to the pan to reach just under the lip of the cups.

5. Bake for about 45 minutes, or until the custards are just set at the edges. They will continue to cook after you remove them from the oven, and the chocolate will harden as it cools. Take care not to overcook; this custard is best when slightly soft. Loosely cover and refrigerate until cold, at least 4 hours.

TO MAKE AHEAD: Refrigerate, covered with plastic wrap, for up to 1 day.

Chocolate Bread Pudding with Sun-Dried Cherries

This bread pudding by Lissa Doumani, chef-owner of Terra in Napa Valley and author of Terra Cooking: From the Heart of Napa Valley, *is given distinction from both the sun-dried cherries and a dose of Cognac. A dollop of tart crème fraîche is needed to balance the richness of the dessert. To plan your schedule keep in mind that you need to dry the bread and soak the cherries overnight. You can make this recipe in a 2-quart soufflé dish or make six 10-ounce individual servings in soufflé dishes.* ♥ SERVES 6

3 cups ¹⁄₂-inch bread cubes from a sourdough bâtarde loaf
   with crusts removed

¹⁄₂ cup sun-dried cherries

¹⁄₃ cup Cognac

8 ounces bittersweet chocolate, chopped

3 large eggs, beaten

1 cup heavy cream

¹⁄₂ cup sour cream or crème fraîche

¹⁄₂ cup sugar

1 teaspoon vanilla extract

¹⁄₈ teaspoon ground cinnamon

1 cup crème fraîche or sour cream

1 tablespoon powdered sugar

6 fresh mint sprigs for garnish

1. Arrange the bread cubes on a baking pan and let sit uncovered overnight to dry. In a small bowl, soak the cherries in the Cognac overnight to soften.

2. Preheat the oven to 350°F.

3. Melt the chocolate in the top of a double boiler set over simmering water, stirring until smooth. Remove from over water. In a large bowl, mix the eggs, cream, sour cream or crème fraîche, sugar, vanilla, and cinnamon until smooth. Whisk in the warm chocolate. Fold in the bread and the cherries with Cognac. Let stand until the bread fully absorbs the custard and no white from the bread is showing. This may take up to 2 hours. Divide the mixture among six 10-ounce individual soufflé dishes or one 2-quart soufflé dish. Place the soufflé dish(es) in a large roasting pan. Fill the pan halfway with boiling water.

4. Bake until the pudding is puffed up and set to the touch, about 35-40 minutes. Carefully remove from the dishes and cool slightly.

5. In a small bowl, whisk the crème fraîche and powdered sugar until soft peaks form. Put a large dollop on top of each serving and garnish with a sprig of mint. Serve warm.

TO MAKE AHEAD: Prepare through Step 4. Let cool completely, cover, and refrigerate for up to 24 hours.
TO REHEAT: Reheat in a preheated 350°F oven for about 6 to 8 minutes before serving. Proceed with Step 5.

Apple Crisp with Dried Fruits

This old-fashioned fruit crisp by Diane Rossen Worthington, from her book American Bistro, *is easy to prepare and will offer homey comfort to all your friends and family.* ❤ SERVES 6

Topping:

1/2 cup plus 2 tablespoons all-purpose flour

1/2 teaspoon ground cinnamon

1/4 teaspoon freshly grated nutmeg

1/4 teaspoon ground allspice

1/8 teaspoon ground cloves

Pinch of salt

1/4 cup coarsely chopped pecans, toasted (see page 93)

3/4 cup old-fashioned rolled oats

1/3 cup granulated sugar

1/2 cup firmly packed dark brown sugar

1/2 cup (1 stick) plus 2 tablespoons cold unsalted butter, cut into small pieces

8 golden delicious apples, about 4 pounds, peeled, cored, and cut into 1/2-inch thick slices

3 tablespoons fresh lemon juice

1/2 cup dried pitted cherries or dried cranberries

1/2 cup sliced dried apricots

1. Preheat the oven to 350°F. Place an oven rack in the center of the oven. Butter a 9-by-13-inch baking dish.

2. To make the topping: In a bowl, stir together the flour, cinnamon, nutmeg, allspice, cloves, and salt. Add the pecans, rolled oats, granulated sugar, brown sugar, and butter. Rub together all the ingredients between your fingertips until they are evenly distributed and the mixture is crumbly and resembles coarse bread crumbs. Set aside.

3. Put the apples in a bowl and toss immediately with the lemon juice, dried cherries, and apricots. Be sure to coat the apples evenly with the lemon juice. Spoon the filling into the prepared dish and sprinkle the topping evenly over the fruit, pressing down lightly and leaving about 1/4 inch between the topping and the rim of the dish.

4. Bake for 40 to 50 minutes, or until the topping is golden brown and bubbling. Cover with aluminum foil if the crust begins to over brown. Remove from the oven and let cool for 15 minutes before serving.

TO MAKE AHEAD: Let cool completely, wrap tightly, and refrigerate for up to 3 days.

TO REHEAT: Reheat, tented with foil, in a preheated 350°F oven for about 15 to 20 minutes.

Buttery Pound Cake

Early recipes for this classic confection literally called for a pound each of flour, butter, sugar, and eggs. This contemporary version by James McNair from James McNair's Cakes *weighs in a bit lighter but equally delicious. For a large pound cake, double the recipe and bake in a 10-inch angel food or other straight-sided tube pan for about 1½ hours. We have also included a few of James's scrumptious variations.* ❤ SERVES 10

Solid vegetable shortening, at room temperature, for greasing

1³/₄ cups all-purpose flour

¹/₂ teaspoon salt

1 cup (2 sticks) unsalted butter, at room temperature

1¹/₂ cups sugar

4 eggs, at room temperature, lightly beaten

3 egg yolks, at room temperature, lightly beaten

2 teaspoons pure vanilla extract

1. Preheat the oven to 325°F. Place an oven rack in the center of the oven. Using a pastry brush, generously grease the bottom and sides of a 9-by-5-inch loaf pan with shortening. Line the bottom with parchment paper, then lightly brush the parchment with shortening and set aside.

2. Place the flour and salt together in a strainer or sifter and sift into a bowl. Whisk to mix well and set aside.

3. In the bowl of a stand mixer fitted with a flat beater, or in a bowl with a hand mixer, beat the butter at medium speed until soft and creamy, about 45 seconds. With the mixer still running, slowly add the sugar, then stop the mixer and scrape the mixture that clings to the sides of the bowl into the center. Continue beating at medium speed until very light and fluffy, about 5 minutes. Slowly

drizzle in the eggs and egg yolks and beat well; stop at least once to scrape the sides of the bowl. Add the vanilla and blend well.

4. Using the mixer on low speed or a rubber spatula, fold in about one-third of the flour mixture, scraping the sides of the bowl and folding just until the flour mixture is incorporated. In the same manner, fold in half of the remaining flour mixture, and finally the remaining flour mixture.

5. Scrape the batter into the prepared pan and smooth the surface with a rubber spatula. Bake until the cake springs back when lightly touched in the center with your fingertip and a wooden skewer inserted into the center of the cake comes out clean, 1 to 1¼ hours.

6. Remove the pan from the oven and place on a wire rack to cool for 5 to 10 minutes. Run the blade of a metal frosting spatula or dull knife around the insides of the pan to loosen the cake. Invert a lightly greased wire rack over the cake, invert the rack and pan together, and lift off the pan. Peel off the parchment. Place another greased rack over the cake and invert to turn upright. Let cool completely.

ALMOND POUND CAKE: Add 7 ounces high-quality packaged almond paste, at room temperature, along with the butter. Add ½ teaspoon pure almond extract along with the vanilla. When the cake comes out of the oven, in a small saucepan, combine ½ cup sugar and ½ cup water. Put over medium-high heat and stir until the sugar is dissolved. Remove from heat and stir in 1 teaspoon pure almond extract. After turning the warm cake out onto the rack, poke the bottom of the cake all over with a wooden skewer and brush or spoon about one-third of the almond syrup over the cake bottom. Turn the cake upright and pierce the top all over with the skewer, then brush or spoon the remaining almond syrup over the top and sides of the cake. Let cool completely, then wrap tightly and store overnight before serving.

CHOCOLATE POUND CAKE: Substitute ½ cup unsweetened cocoa for an equal amount of the flour. After the cake is cooled completely, spoon a chocolate glaze over the top, if desired.

PEANUT BUTTER POUND CAKE: Beat in ½ cup creamy peanut butter along with the butter.

TO MAKE AHEAD: For optimal flavor, eat the cake within 2 days of baking. Wrap tightly with aluminum foil and store at room temperature for up to 2 days. Freeze, tightly wrapped in plastic wrap, for up to two weeks. Thaw in the refrigerator or at room temperature before serving.

Glazed Cinnamon Rolls

This recipe from The Bread Bible *by Beth Hensperger resides at the apex of the cinnamon roll world. They are at their best the day they are made, but you can freeze a batch once they are cool, and their light texture will be preserved.* ♥ MAKES 18 ROLLS

Dough:

1 russet potato (about 6 ounces), peeled and cut into
    large chunks

2 tablespoons unsalted butter

$\frac{1}{4}$ cup warm water (105° to 115°F)

1 package active dry yeast

$\frac{1}{2}$ cup granulated sugar, or $\frac{1}{3}$ cup (packed) light brown sugar

2 tablespoons canola or nut oil

1 large egg, at room temperature

1 teaspoon salt

5 to $5\frac{1}{2}$ cups unbleached all-purpose flour

Filling:

4 tablespoons ($\frac{1}{2}$ stick) unsalted butter, melted

$1\frac{1}{4}$ cups packed light brown sugar

$1\frac{1}{2}$ tablespoons ground cinnamon

1 cup dark raisins or dried currants, plumped in hot water
    10 minutes and drained (optional)

1 cup (4 ounces) walnuts or pecans, toasted (see page 93) and
    coarsely chopped (optional)

Glaze:

$1\frac{1}{2}$ cups sifted confectioners' sugar

4 to 5 tablespoons Irish cream liqueur or milk

1. In a medium saucepan, combine the potato chunks with water to cover. Bring to a boil, reduce the heat to low, and cook, uncovered, until tender, about 20 minutes. Drain the potato, reserving 1 cup of the liquid. Let the potato water cool to 105° to 115°F. Meanwhile, process the potato with the butter through a food mill placed over a bowl or puree it in a food processor fitted with the metal blade just until smooth. This produces ¾ to 1 cup of puree.

2. Pour the warm water in a small bowl. Sprinkle the yeast and a pinch of the granulated or brown sugar over the surface of the water. Stir to dissolve and let stand at room temperature until foamy, about 10 minutes.

3. In a large bowl with a whisk or in the work bowl of a heavy-duty electric mixer fitted with the paddle attachment, combine the pureed potato, reserved warm potato water, yeast mixture, remaining granulated or brown sugar, oil, egg, salt, and 2 cups of the flour. Beat hard to combine, about 1 minute. Add the remaining flour, ½ cup at a time, until a shaggy dough that just clears the sides of the bowl is formed.

4. Turn the dough out onto a lightly floured work surface and knead until smooth and springy, about 4 to 6 minutes if kneading by hand. If kneading with dough hook or electric mixer, knead 4 minutes on

continued

medium speed. Dust with flour 1 tablespoon at a time as needed to prevent sticking. Take care not to add too much flour, because the dough should be very satiny.

5. Put the dough in a greased deep container. Turn once to coat the top and cover the bowl with plastic wrap. Let rise in a warm place until doubled in bulk, about 1 hour. Gently deflate the dough and let rise a second time until doubled in bulk, 50 minutes to 1 hour.

6. Preheat the oven to 350°F. Place an oven rack in the middle of the oven. Line a baking sheet with parchment paper.

7. Gently deflate the dough and turn it out onto a lightly floured work surface. Divide the dough into 2 equal portions. Roll out each portion into a 10-by-14-inch rectangle at least ¼ inch thick. Brush the surface of each rectangle with the melted butter. Sprinkle the surface of each rectangle evenly with half of the brown sugar and cinnamon, leaving a 1-inch border around the edges. Sprinkle with the raisins or currants and nuts, if using. Starting from the long side, roll the dough up jelly-roll fashion. Pinch the seams together and, using a serrated knife or dental floss, cut each roll crosswise into 9 equal portions, each 1 to 1½ inches thick. Place each portion cut side up on the prepared pan at least 2 inches apart. Press gently to flatten each swirl slightly. (Alternatively, place in 18 greased 3-inch muffin-pan cups for a top-knot effect.) Cover loosely with plastic wrap and let rise at room temperature just until puffy, 20 to 30 minutes.

8. Put the baking sheet or muffin cups in the center of the oven and bake 25 to 30 minutes, or until golden brown and firm to the touch. Using a metal spatula, transfer to a wire rack. Immediately prepare the glaze by combining the confectioners' sugar and liqueur or milk in a small mixing bowl and whisking until smooth. Adjust the consistency of the glaze by adding more liqueur or milk, a few drops at a time, to make a pourable mixture. Dip your fingers or a large spoon into the glaze and drizzle it over the rolls by running your hand or the spoon back and forth over the tops. Or, apply the glaze to the rolls with a brush. Let sit until just warm before eating.

TO MAKE AHEAD: Dough may be made ahead and refrigerated overnight, covered with a double layer of plastic wrap. Let stand at room temperature 3 to 4 hours before filling and rising. Once made, the buns can be stored at room temperature for up to 3 days or freeze in self-sealing freezer bags for up to 3 months.

Mrs. Keller's Gingerbread

This recipe for an old-fashioned treat, which Sara Perry featured in her book Great Gingerbread, *was penned by her friend Mary Ellen Buck in 1905. Rich, dark, and moist, this not-too-sweet heirloom gingerbread gets its traditional flavor from blackstrap molasses, the thickest, darkest, and most concentrated grade of molasses.* ♥ SERVES 12

½ cup (1 stick) unsalted butter, at room temperature

1 cup sugar (see Note)

1 cup blackstrap molasses

2 large eggs, well beaten

2½ cups all-purpose flour

1 tablespoon ground ginger

1 teaspoon ground cinnamon

1 teaspoon ground cloves

1 cup boiling water

2 teaspoons baking soda

Sweetened whipped cream for serving (optional)

1. Preheat the oven to 350°F. Place an oven rack in the center of the oven. Grease a 9-by-13-inch baking pan.

2. In a large bowl, beat the butter and sugar together until light and creamy. Stir in the molasses until smooth. Stir in the eggs until well combined.

3. Sift the flour, ginger, cinnamon, and cloves into the molasses mixture, and beat until smooth.

4. In a small bowl, combine the boiling water and baking soda. The mixture will be foamy. Slowly add the soda mixture to the batter, stirring until well combined. Check to make sure the butter is blended and uniform. Pour the batter into the prepared pan.

5. Bake until a toothpick inserted in the middle comes out clean, about 50 minutes. Cool in the pan on a wire rack for 5 minutes before cutting into squares. Serve warm, with whipped cream, if desired.

NOTE: For those who prefer a sweeter cake, increase the sugar by ½ cup or substitue dark or light molasses.

TO MAKE AHEAD: Let cool completely, wrap tightly, and store at room temperature for up to 3 days, or freeze in a self-sealing freezer bag for up to 1 month. Thaw, wrapped, at room temperature.

Poached Pears with Orange Sauce

Tucked upright in a simple container these flavorful pears presented by Sara Perry in Christmastime Treats *are perfect for any-one who is looking for a low-fat, light dessert. The pears can be served warm, at room temperature, or chilled.* ♥ SERVES 6

½ cup apple cider

½ cup water

1½ cups sugar

Zest of 2 oranges, finely minced or grated

Zest of 1 lemon, finely minced or grated

3 tablespoons fresh lemon juice

6 firm pears such as Comice or Bosc

1 cup fresh orange juice

¾ cup mascarpone cheese

6 tablespoons minced crystallized ginger

1. In a saucepan large enough to hold the upright pears without crowding, combine the apple cider, water, sugar, orange and lemon zests, and lemon juice. Place over medium heat and cook, stirring often, until the sugar dissolves and the mixture comes to a boil. Remove from the heat and set aside.

2. Peel the pears, leaving the stems attached. If necessary, cut a thin sliver off the bottoms so they will stand upright. Place the pears upright in the pan. With a bulb baster or a spoon, drizzle each pear with the syrup. Cover and bring to a simmer over medium-high heat. Cook, basting frequently with the syrup, until the pears can be easily pierced with the tip of a sharp knife, 20 to 25 minutes. Remove from heat. With a slotted spoon, transfer the pears to a shallow serving platter.

3. Pour the poaching syrup through a fine-mesh sieve placed over a pitcher. Reserve the zest to use as a garnish. Measure 1 cup syrup and pour it into a small saucepan. (Reserve and chill the remaining syrup for use in other recipes.) Add the orange juice to the saucepan and stir to mix. Place over medium heat, bring to a gentle boil, and boil until reduced to a thick syrup, about 20 minutes. Remove from heat and let cool until just warm. Drizzle 1 tablespoon of the warm sauce over each pear.

4. To serve, arrange the pears on individual plates. Place a spoonful of mascarpone next to each pear and spoon the remaining sauce over each pear. Garnish each pear with some of the reserved zest. Garnish each spoonful of mascarpone with 1 tablespoon of the minced ginger and a few flecks of the remaining zest.

TO MAKE AHEAD: The pears can be poached up to 4 hours ahead and kept at room temperature. The pears will keep, refrigerated in an airtight container, for up to 1 day.

Mile-High Lemon Angel Food Cake with Lemon Glaze

Although angel food cake probably derives from an English recipe, most Americans think of it as a national classic, like strawberry shortcake. Instead of lemon juice or lemon zest, Lori Longbotham uses pure lemon oil in this version, from her book Luscious Lemon Desserts, *which results in an intense, vibrant, and wonderful lemon flavor. This cake is better the day after it's made, so it's a great recipe to make ahead. Serve it topped with Lemon Glaze, or try it lightly toasted for breakfast—either way, it's delicious.* ❤ SERVES 8 TO 10

1 cup cake flour (not self-rising), sifted

$^3/_4$ cup confectioners' sugar

14 egg whites, at room temperature

1$^1/_2$ teaspoons cream of tartar

$^1/_4$ teaspoon salt

$^3/_4$ cup granulated sugar

2 teaspoons pure vanilla extract

1 teaspoon pure lemon oil

Lemon Glaze:

1 cup confectioners' sugar

2 tablespoons fresh lemon juice

1$^1/_2$ teaspoons grated lemon zest

Pinch of salt

1. Preheat the oven to 375°F. Place an oven rack in the center of the oven. Have ready an ungreased 10-inch tube pan.

2. Sift the flour and the confectioners' sugar together into a medium bowl.

3. Beat the egg whites with an electric mixer on medium speed in a large bowl until foamy. Increase the speed to medium-high, add the cream of tartar and salt, and beat just until the egg whites form soft peaks. Add the granulated sugar, about 1 tablespoon at a time, beating well after each addition, and beat just until the whites form stiff, glossy peaks. Add the vanilla and lemon oil and beat until well combined.

4. Sift one-fourth of the flour mixture over the egg whites and fold in with a whisk or a rubber spatula. Continue gently folding, one quarter at a time, until all the flour mixture has been added, being careful not to overmix.

5. Transfer the batter to the pan. Run a table knife through the batter to remove any large air pockets, and smooth the top with a rubber spatula. Bake for 35 to 40 minutes, until the top is golden brown and the cake pulls away from the side of the pan. Turn the pan upside down, and balance it on its elongated neck or pan legs (it if has them), or hang the tube upside down from the neck of a tall bottle. Let cool to room temperature.

6. Turn the pan right side up. Run a knife around the outside edge of the cake and between the cake and the tube. Top the cake with a flat plate, invert it, give a sharp downward rap to the pan to dislodge the cake, and lift off the pan. If the pan bottom is removable, slide a knife between the pan bottom and the cake to release it.

7. To make the glaze: Stir the ingredients together in a small bowl. Let stand for 10 minutes before using.

Pour it over the cake and let stand for at least 10 minutes, or until the glaze is set.

8. Use a sharp serrated knife to cut the cake into wedges.

TO MAKE AHEAD: Let cool completely, wrap tightly, and store at room temperature for up to 3 days, or freeze in a self-sealing freezer bag for up to 2 weeks.

Oatmeal-Raisin Cookies

As cozy as a country kitchen, oatmeal cookies are, as James McNair and Andrew Moore call them in this recipe from their book Afternoon Delights, *the traditional comfort cookie. Their version uses lots of old-fashioned rolled oats for maximum chewiness. Although typically made with raisins, dried cranberries or blueberries or chopped dried sour cherries can be used instead.*

♥ MAKES ABOUT 1 DOZEN LARGE COOKIES

1/2 cup all-purpose flour

1/2 teaspoon baking soda

1/2 teaspoon salt

3/4 cup (1 1/2 sticks) unsalted butter, at room temperature

1 cup firmly packed light brown sugar

1/2 cup granulated sugar

1 large egg, at room temperature

2 teaspoons pure vanilla extract

3 cups old-fashioned (not quick-cooking) rolled oats

1 cup raisins

1. Preheat the oven to 350°F. Place an oven rack in the middle of the oven. Line a baking sheet with parchment paper and set aside.

2. In a medium bowl, combine the flour, baking soda, and salt. Whisk to mix well and set aside.

3. In a large bowl, combine the butter and sugars and beat with an electric mixer at medium speed until the mixture is light and fluffy, about 5 minutes. Add the egg and vanilla and blend well. Add the flour mixture and mix at low speed just until incorporated, scraping down the sides as needed. Stir in the oats, about 1 cup at a time, just until incorporated, then stir in the raisins.

4. Using a No. 20 (1/4-cup) ice-cream scoop, scoop up level portions of the dough and place them about 3 inches apart on the prepared pan until the sheet is full.

(Cover the remaining dough tightly with plastic wrap to prevent drying out and set aside until forming the next batch of cookies.)

5. Bake until the edges of the cookies are lightly browned and the centers are set, about 18 minutes.

6. Transfer the baking sheet to a wire rack to cool for a few minutes, then, using a spatula, transfer the cookies directly to the rack and let cool completely.

7. Repeat to use the remaining dough.

TO MAKE AHEAD: Prepare through Step 3 up to 3 hours ahead, cover, and refrigerate for up to 2 days, or prepare through Step 4 and freeze scoops of dough in self-sealing freezer bags for up to 1 month. After baking, store the cookies in airtight containers for up to 3 days.

Chocolate Chip Cookies

This cookie recipe by Peggy Cullen from Got Milk? The Cookie Book, *is pretty much the perfect chocolate chip cookie: soft, chewy, crisp, and crunchy all at once. Peggy likes to make up the dough and freeze 1½-inch balls in self-sealing bags. She can then bake the dough right out of the freezer for hot chocolate chip cookies anytime.* ♥ MAKES ABOUT 2½ DOZEN COOKIES

½ cup (1 stick) unsalted butter, at room temperature

6 tablespoons granulated sugar

6 tablespoons packed light brown sugar

¼ teaspoon salt

1½ teaspoons vanilla extract

1 large egg

1 cup plus 2 tablespoons all-purpose flour

½ teaspoon baking soda

1 cup (6 ounces) chocolate chunks or chips

1 cup (about 4 ounces) large pecan or walnut pieces,
    or any nut you prefer

1. Preheat the oven to 375°F. Place an oven rack in the middle of the oven.

2. In a medium bowl, using an electric mixer, beat the butter, sugars, salt, and vanilla until well combined. Beat in the egg. Scrape down the bowl using a rubber spatula, and beat for a few more seconds.

3. In a small bowl, whisk together the flour and baking soda. Add the dry ingredients to the wet mixture and mix on low speed just until blended. Combine the chocolate chunks and nuts in a small bowl and stir into the dough.

4. Shape the dough into 1½-inch balls and drop them about 3 inches apart onto ungreased baking sheets. For perfectly uniform cookies, scoop the dough using a 1½-inch-diameter ice-cream scoop, leveling the dough off across the top before dropping onto the baking sheets. Bake for 9 to 12 minutes, or until the edges are golden. Remove from the oven, let sit for 5 minutes, then transfer the cookies to wire racks to cool completely.

TO MAKE AHEAD: Prepare through Step 3 up to 3 hours ahead, cover, and refrigerate for up to 2 days, or prepare through Step 4, except for baking, and freeze scoops of dough in self-sealing freezer bags for up to 1 month. After baking, store the cookies in airtight containers for up to 3 days.

S'more Squares

You don't need a campfire to make this version of the classic s'more from Sweet Miniatures *by Flo Braker. It has all the luscious ingredients in a petit-four-sized morsel.* ♥ MAKES ABOUT 4 DOZEN 1½-INCH SQUARES

Crust:

1½ cups graham cracker crumbs

¼ cup packed light brown sugar

7 tablespoons unsalted butter, melted

Filling:

⅔ cup unsifted all-purpose flour

¼ teaspoon salt

⅛ teaspoon baking soda

2 ounces unsweetened chocolate, chopped

6 tablespoons unsalted butter

1 tablespoon water

1 cup granulated sugar

2 large eggs

2 teaspoons pure vanilla extract

Topping:

2 ounces milk chocolate, melted

4 dozen mini marshmallows

1. Preheat the oven to 325°F. Place an oven rack in the lower third of the oven. Fit a sheet of aluminum foil to the bottom and sides of a 9-inch square pan. Invert the pan and gently press the aluminum form into the pan to fit the contours.

2. To make the crust: In a large bowl, blend the graham cracker crumbs and the sugar. Add the butter and blend thoroughly. Press the crumbs into the foil-lined pan and set aside.

3. To make the filling: Sift the flour, salt, and baking soda onto a piece of waxed paper. In a small saucepan, melt the chocolate and butter over low heat, stirring occasionally. Turn off heat and stir in the water. Pour the mixture into a large bowl and let cool for about 5 minutes. Stir in the sugar, then the eggs and vanilla, just until blended. Add the flour mixture, stirring just until combined. Pour the filling into the crumb-lined pan, spreading evenly.

4. Bake for 30 minutes only. Remove from the oven and transfer the pan to a wire rack. Let cool completely.

continued

5. To make the topping: Transfer the cake from the pan to a cutting board by lifting the foil by its edges. Cut a 6-inch square of parchment paper and roll it into a cone. Tape the sides closed and cut off the tip of the cone to make a small opening. Pour the chocolate into the cone and pipe zigzag lines over the filling. Cut the cookies into 1½-inch squares. Center a mini marshmallow on each square, and pipe a tiny dot of chocolate in the center of each marshmallow.

TO MAKE AHEAD: Store at room temperature in one layer in a covered foil-lined cardboard container, such as a cake box, for up to 2 days.

Double-Fudge Frosted Brownies

These brownies by Tish Boyle from Diner Desserts *have a double benefit—they are loaded with chocolate (an instant mood elevator) and are easily transported for gift giving or sharing with friends (a good way to score brownie points). Tish also likes to bring these brownies along when she's invited to dinner (sometimes she think that's the reason she's invited). The brownies freeze well, so you can always have a supply on hand.* ♥ MAKES 9 BROWNIES

½ cup (1 stick) unsalted butter, cut into tablespoons

½ cup lightly packed light brown sugar

6 ounces semisweet chocolate, chopped

2 ounces unsweetened chocolate, chopped

¼ cup granulated sugar

3 large eggs

1½ teaspoons vanilla extract

½ cup all-purpose flour

¼ teaspoon salt

Frosting:

3 tablespoons unsalted butter, cut into tablespoons

2 ounces unsweetened chocolate, chopped

1 ounce milk chocolate, chopped

1½ cups confectioners' sugar, sifted

Pinch of salt

¼ cup heavy cream

1 teaspoon vanilla extract

¼ cup chopped walnuts for garnish (optional)

1. Preheat the oven to 350°F. Line an 8-inch square baking pan with aluminum foil so that the foil extends 2 inches beyond two opposite sides of the pan. Lightly butter the bottom and sides of the foil-lined pan.

2. In a medium saucepan, combine the butter pieces, brown sugar, and semisweet and unsweetened chocolates. Cook over low heat, stirring constantly, until the butter and chocolates melt and the mixture is smooth. Transfer to a medium bowl.

3. With a wooden spoon, stir in the granulated sugar. Stir in the eggs, one at a time, until there is no trace of yolk. Mix in the vanilla. Add the flour and salt and mix vigorously until the mixture is shiny and smooth. Scrape the batter into the prepared pan and smooth the top with a rubber spatula.

4. Bake the brownies for 35 to 40 minutes, or until a toothpick inserted into the center comes out with a few moist crumbs clinging to it. Do not overbake. Remove from the oven and transfer the pan to a wire rack. Let cool for 45 minutes. Using the 2 ends of the foil as handles, lift the brownies out of the pan. Invert onto the wire rack and peel off the foil. Let cool completely (the brownies will be frosted on the smooth side).

5. To make the frosting: Place the butter and both types of chocolate in a medium saucepan. Heat over very low heat, stirring constantly, until the chocolates melt and the mixture is smooth. Transfer to the bowl of an electric mixer. On low speed, add half of the confectioners' sugar, the salt, and then half of the cream. Blend in the remaining confectioners' sugar and the remaining cream. Beat in the vanilla extract. Beat the frosting on medium speed for 30 seconds, or until smooth and shiny.

6. Spread the frosting over the uncut brownies, making it as smooth as possible. Garnish the top with chopped walnuts, if desired. Cut into 9 squares and serve at room temperature.

TO MAKE AHEAD: Wrap each brownie in plastic wrap and refrigerate for up to 5 days, or put the wrapped brownies in self-sealing freezer bags and freeze for up to 1 month. Bring to room temperature before serving, for maximum flavor impact.

CHAPTER 6

Healing Tonics and Elixirs

Teas, tonics, and smoothies are a wonderful antidote to whatever ails anyone. The range of teas, tonics, and elixirs include such healing and soothing ingredients as ginger, chamomile, and honey. Luscious fruit smoothies make healthy milkshakes, full of vitamins and minerals for rejuvenation. Bring tea in a hot thermos, brew it at your destination, or make up a gift basket with a beautiful teacup, tea canister, or teapot to accompany your tea blend, and put elixirs in elegant stoppered glass bottles. Serve smoothies immediately in a thermos or freeze them in ziplock bags for easily delivery.

Citrus Remedy

Here is a quick and easy recipe from Wise Concoctions *by Bonnie Trust Dahan. It delivers a concentrated dose of bioflavonoids, which act as natural anti-inflammatories to reduce the swelling of tissues and ease the severity of allergy symptoms.*

♥ MAKES 3 CUPS

Peels from 3 grapefruits, finely minced
    (a food processor makes this easy)
Peels from 3 lemons, fincly minced

$1\frac{1}{2}$ cups purified water
$\frac{1}{2}$ to $\frac{3}{4}$ cup local honey

1. Put the minced peels and water in a saucepan. Cover and simmer for 20 minutes. Stir in the honey to taste when slightly cooled. Use 1 teaspoon 3 times per day.

TO MAKE AHEAD: Store in a glass jar with a lid in the refrigerator for up to 1 week.

Herbal Ginger Brew

Ginger has been considered a therapeutic herb for at least two thousand years, and its digestive and antispasmodic properties have led to its reputation as an effective antidote for stomach cramps, indigestion, flatulence, and nausea. Its warming qualities also make it an excellent circulatory and energy stimulant. This recipe from Wise Concoctions, *which Bonnie Trust Dahan learned from herbalist Diana DeLuca, makes a delicious and healthy alternative to store-bought, overly sweetened ginger ales.* ❤ SERVES 1

Ginger Syrup:

1/2 cup peeled and sliced fresh ginger

1 cup purified water

1/4 cup pure maple syrup

1 cup carbonated mineral water

1 tablespoon fresh squeezed lemon juice

1 strip of lemon peel

1. To make the Ginger Syrup: Combine the sliced ginger and water and simmer for 30 minutes. Cool slightly, then strain. Add the maple syrup and stir to mix. You should have about a cup of syrup.

2. Stir 2 tablespoons of the syrup into the carbonated water until thoroughly mixed; refrigerate the remainder of the syrup for later use. Add the lemon juice and stir. Garnish with the lemon peel.

TO MAKE AHEAD: The Ginger Syrup will keep in the refrigerator for up to 6 months.

Rosemary Rejuvenating Tonic

Rosemary, one of the earliest herbs to be recorded for use in medicine, is a superb rejuvenation herb. Thyme is prized for its antiseptic properties. Combined with lemon, both herbs provide an invigorating tonic guaranteed to increase energy. This recipe, which comes from Well Being *by Barbara Close, has a tonifying effect on both the circulatory and the digestive systems, but its main impact is on the nervous system, where it acts as a stimulant. Rosemary is traditionally known as a memory enhancer, and legend tells us that Greek students wore rosemary necklaces to improve their concentration. Relate this story on a note to give along with the tonic.* ♥ MAKES 4 CUPS

3 teaspoons fresh rosemary leaves, broken into small pieces

1 teaspoon fresh thyme leaves

1-inch piece fresh ginger, thinly sliced

$^1/_2$ lemon, thinly sliced

4 cups purified water, boiled

$^1/_2$ cup honey

1. Put the rosemary, thyme, ginger, and lemon in a French press. Add the hot water and stir. Steep for 10 minutes and strain. Sweeten with honey and serve hot or cold.

Rest and Refresh Tea

Sara Perry, who includes this herbal tea blend in The Book of Herbal Teas, *calls the flavorful combination the perfect afternoon pick-me-up. The chamomile has a restful quality and its taste is applelike, while the basil and citrus peels refresh with their peppery zing. You can prepare the blend ahead of time and give small packets as healing gifts.* ♥ MAKES 2 CUPS TEA BLEND

¹/₂ cup dried chamomile flowers

¹/₄ cup dried basil leaves

2 tablespoons dried peppermint leaves

2 tablespoons dried lemon peel

2 tablespoons dried orange peel

1. Put all of the ingredients in a quart-sized plastic bag. Blow into the bag as if blowing up a balloon. Once it's inflated, hold the bag shut and shake until well combined. Store in a clean, opaque glass or ceramic jar with a screw-top lid or tight-fitting cork. Give the jar a good shake to help distribute the different ingredients before removing any tea for brewing.

2. To use, measure 1 rounded teaspoon for each 6- to 8-ounce cup of freshly boiled water. Steep for 5 to 6 minutes.

Hot Honey Lemonade

Flannel jammies, a stack of magazines, and a big mug of steaming-hot honey lemonade is our answer to winter's annual siege of colds and flu. This comforting, delicious brew, from Stephanie Rosenbaum's Honey: From Flower to Table, *is full of cold-busting vitamin C, with plenty of honey to soothe a sore throat. If you live in an area where Meyer lemons thrive, use them to make an extra-sweet and fragrant drink.* ❤ SERVES 1

2 lemons

3 or 4 whole cloves

2 tablespoons honey, or to taste

1 cup boiling water

1 cinnamon stick

1. Squeeze the juice of 1 lemon into a large mug. Slice the second lemon very thinly. Poke the cloves into a lemon slice, and drop the slices into the mug. Add the honey. Fill the cup with the hot water and stir with the cinnamon stick until the honey has dissolved. Taste for sweetness and add more honey as you like.

NOTE: In a pinch, you can make this drink with bottled lemon juice. Use 2 tablespoons of lemon juice and increase the honey to 2½ tablespoons, as bottled juice is more bitter than fresh.

Stomach Soother Smoothie

Sara Whiteford and Mary Barber created this comforting smoothie to help tame an out-of-sorts tummy. The combination of fresh fruits and green tea makes a surprisingly refreshing drink. ❤ SERVES 2

¼ cup strong-brewed green tea, chilled

1 cup diced apricots

¼ cup mango sorbet

2 tablespoons frozen pineapple juice concentrate

1 teaspoon fresh lime juice

¼ teaspoon grated fresh ginger

1. Combine the green tea and apricots in a blender. Add all the remaining ingredients and blend until smooth.

TO MAKE AHEAD: Freeze in plastic ziplock bags for up to 1 week. Thaw for 30 to 45 minutes before serving.

Flu-Buster Smoothie

In Super Smoothies, Sara Whiteford and Mary Barber describe this terrific drink as custom-made for those stuffy-head, runny-nose, feeling-lousy kind of days. The orange juice, strawberries, and papaya deliver a triple dose of vitamin C. Drink a tall glass at bedtime and you won't need to call the doctor in the morning. ♥ SERVES 2

1 cup fresh orange juice

1 cup quartered fresh strawberries

³/₄ cup diced papaya

1 frozen banana, sliced

1. Combine the orange juice and strawberries in a blender. Add the papaya and banana. Blend until smooth.

TO MAKE AHEAD: Freeze in plastic self-sealing bags for up to 1 week. Thaw for 30 to 45 minutes before serving.

C-Breeze Smoothie

The combination of kiwi and cantaloupe in this shake offers a whopping 230 percent of the recommended daily allowance for vitamin C, along with 80 percent of the RDA for vitamin A. That combination could mean death to your next cold. This smoothie from Super Smoothies by Sara Whiteford and Mary Barber tastes delightfully similar to the Sweet Tart candies they loved as kids. If your kiwis are really ripe and sweet, you may want to add a squeeze of fresh lime juice. ♥ SERVES 2

1 cup diced kiwi (about 3), chilled

1 cup orange sherbet

1³/₄ cups diced cantaloupe, chilled

1. Combine all the ingredients in a food processor. Process until smooth.

TO MAKE AHEAD: Freeze in self-sealing bags for up to 1 week. Thaw for 30 to 45 minutes before serving.

Author Biographies

AYLA ALGAR teaches Turkish language at UC Berkeley. She is the author of *Classical Turkish Cooking.*

Twin sisters MARY BARBER and SARA WHITEFORD, former chefs and caterers, are culinary consultants and the authors of *Smoothies, Wraps, Cocktail Food,* and *Super Smoothies,* all published by Chronicle Books. They live in San Francisco.

TISH BOYLE is the food editor for *Chocolatier* and *Pastry Art & Design* magazines. She is the author of *Diner Desserts* (Chronicle Books). She lives in Brooklyn Heights, New York.

FLO BRAKER is widely acknowledged as a preeminent baking expert as well as a popular television presence and a columnist for the *San Francisco Chronicle.* She is the author of *The Simple Art of Perfect Baking* and *Sweet Miniatures* (Chronicle Books). She lives in Palo Alto, California.

GEORGEANNE BRENNAN is a James Beard–award winning cookbook author and teacher who divides her time between her small farm in Northern California and her home in Provence, where she runs a cooking school. Her previous books include *Potager: Fresh Garden Cooking in the French Style; The Mediterranean Herb Cookbook; The Vegetarian Table: France; The Food and Flavors of Haute Provence;* and *Olives, Anchovies, and Capers;* all published by Chronicle Books.

MICHAEL CHIARELLO is a cookbook author, and vintner, and the founder of Napa Style, a line of specialty products. He is the host of the PBS series *Michael Chiraello's Napa,* a frequent contributor to the *CBS Early Show,* and the author of *The Tra Vigne Cookbook,* and *Michael Chiarello's Casual Cooking,* both published by Chronicle Books.

BARBARA CLOSE is a certified aromatherapist and the owner and founder of Naturopathica, a holistic spa in East Hampton, New York. She is the author of *Aromatherapy: The A–Z Guide to Healing with Essential Oils,* as well as *Well Being* and *The Spa Deck,* both published by Chronicle Books.

PEGGY CULLEN is a writer, baker, and candy maker. She is the author of *Got Milk? The Cookie Book* (Chronicle Books), as well as a frequent contributor to food magazines. She lives in Western Massachusetts.

MARION CUNNINGHAM, the "Lost Recipes" columnist for the *San Francisco Chronicle,* lives in Walnut Creek, California, and is known as the modern-day Fannie Farmer. She is the author of two revisions of *The Fannie Farmer Cookbook,* as well as *The Supper Book, Cooking with Children,* and *Learning to Cook with Marion Cunningham.*

BONNIE TRUST DAHAN first discovered herbal healing while traveling in Morocco twenty-five years ago. She is the founder of PureSeasons, a company dedicated to natural living and style. Her previous books include *Wise Concoctions, Garden House,* and *Garden Home: City,* all published by Chronicle Books.

JULIA DELLA CROCE is a James Beard Foundation Award–winning cookbook author, journalist, lecturer, and teacher. Some of her previous books include *Pasta Classica, The Pasta Book, Antipasti,* and *The Vegetarian Table: Italy,* all published by Chronicle Books.

JODY DENTON is a veteran of some of the nation's top restaurants. Most recently, he was executive chef and partner of the San Francisco Bay Area restaurants LuLu, Azie, and Zibibbo. He now has his own restaurant, Merenda, in Bend, Oregon.

LISSA DOUMANI was a pastry chef at Spago and 385 North in Los Angeles before she left to launch the Napa Valley restaurant Terra with her husband Hiro Sone. She is the author of *Terra: Cooking from the Heart of Napa Valley.*

JEANNETTE FERRARY is the author of *M. F. K. Fisher and Me: A Memoir of Food and Friendship.* With Louise Fiszer she is the author of *A Good Day for Soup, A Good Day for Salad,* and *Jewish Holiday Feasts,* all from Chronicle Books. She lives in California and teaches food writing at UC Berkeley.

LOUISE FISZER, a nationally known cooking teacher, food writer, and consultant, owned and directed one of Northern California's most popular cooking schools for fifteen years. With Jeannette Ferrary she is the author of six books, including *A Good Day for Soup, A Good Day for Salad,* and *Jewish Holiday Feasts,* all published by Chronicle Books.

JANET FLETCHER, trained at the Culinary Institute of America and a veteran of Berkeley's celebrated Chez Panisse restaurant, is a *San Francisco Chronicle* staff food writer. She has authored or co-authored fourteen books on food and wine, including *The Cheese Course, Fresh from the Farmers' Market,* and *Pasta Harvest,* all published by Chronicle Books.

DAVID GARRIDO helped pioneer Southwestern cuisine in Texas. He is the executive chef at Jeffrey's Restaurants (in Austin, Texas, and in Washington, D.C.) and at Cipollina in Austin, Texas. He is the co-author, with Robb Walsh, of *Nuevo Tex-Mex,* published by Chronicle Books.

JOYCE GOLDSTEIN is a nationally known chef, author, teacher, and Mediterranean-cooking expert. The former chef-owner of the award-winning Square One restaurant, she is the author of *Cucina Ebraica, Sephardic Flavors,* and *Enoteca,* all published by Chronicle Books, as well as the classics *The Mediterranean Kitchen* and *Back to Square One.* She lives in San Francisco.

LAUREN GROVEMAN is a professional cooking instructor, a working wife and mother, and a noted food writer. She is the host of the public television series *Home Cooking with Lauren Groveman,* as well as the James Beard Award–winning radio program *Food, Family & Home "Matters" with Lauren Groveman.* She is the author of *Lauren Groveman's Kitchen,* published by Chronicle Books, and lives in Larchmont, New York.

SAM GUGINO is the author of *Cooking to Beat the Clock* and *Low-Fat Cooking to Beat the Clock,* both from Chronicle Books. A former restaurateur turned food journalist, he has been the restaurant critic at the *Philadelphia Daily News* and the food editor for the *San Jose Mercury News,* and is also the "Tastes" columnist for the *Wine Spectator.*

BETH HENSPERGER has spent more than three decades exploring baking traditions, both ancient and modern, around the world. Her fourteen cookbooks include *The Bread Bible* and *The Pleasures of Whole Grain Breads* (both published by Chronicle Books), as well as *The Best Quick Breads* and *The Bread Lover's Bread Machine Cookbook.*

GERALD HIRIGOYEN is executive chef and co-owner of the restaurants Fringale and Pastis in San Francisco. He is the recipient of numerous awards and is also the author of *Bistro* and *The Basque Kitchen.*

HUBERT KELLER is the executive chef and co-owner of San Francisco's restaurant Fleur de Lys. His cooking has been praised in *Esquire,* the *New York Times,* and *Food & Wine.* He is the author of *The Cuisine of Hubert Keller.*

LORETTA KELLER studied in France and worked at Bistro at the Maison de Ville in New Orleans. She opened her own restaurant, Bizou, in San Francisco in 1993, which has been praised in the *San Francisco Chronicle* and *Gourmet.*

PEGGY KNICKERBOCKER is a freelance food and travel writer who lives in San Francisco. She is also a cooking teacher. She is the author of *Olive Oil,* published by Chronicle Books, and the co-author of *The Rose Pistola Cookbook.*

BARBARA LAUTERBACH is a spokesperson for King Arthur Flour, as well as a cooking teacher and author who contributes to national magazines. She is the author of *Potato Salad,* published by Chronicle Books.

LORI LONGBOTHAM is a former food editor for *Gourmet* and contributes articles to a variety of magazines. She lives in the New York City area and is the author of *Luscious Lemon Desserts,* published by Chronicle Books.

DONATA MAGGIPINTO is the culinary and editorial director for Williams-Sonoma and a regular contributor to NBC's *Today* show. She is the author of *Real-Life Entertaining* and *Halloween Treats* (Chronicle Books). She lives in Northern California.

NANCIE MCDERMOTT, a well-known expert on Thai food, has written numerous newspaper and magazine articles on Thai cooking, and teaches courses on the subject at cooking schools around the country. She is the author of *Real Thai* and *Real Vegetarian Thai,* both published by Chronicle Books.

JAMES MCNAIR is the author of forty popular cookbooks that have sold almost four million copies. He is best known for titles such as *Chicken, Cold Pasta,* and *Salmon,* all published by Chronicle Books. He lives in Napa Valley and at Lake Tahoe.

DIANE MORGAN writes a column for the *Los Angeles Times* and is the author of *The Thanksgiving Table, Cooking for the Week* (with Dan Taggart and Kathleen Taggart), and *Dressed to Grill* (with Karen Brooks and Reed Darmon), all published by Chronicle Books. She lives in Portland, Oregon.

JEFF MORGAN, wine director for Dean & DeLuca, is the author of *Dean & Deluca: The Food and Wine Cookbook* (Chronicle Books). He has written on wine, food, and agriculture for numerous publications including the *New York Times* and *Wine Spectator* (as its West Coast editor). He is also a Napa Valley–based wine maker and produces Solo Rosa, a barrell-fermented dry rosé.

KITTY MORSE was born in Casablanca, Morocco. She has taught Moroccan cooking for over twenty years and is the author of numerous cookbooks, among them *Cooking at the Kasbah, Couscous,* and *Vegetarian Table: North Africa,* all from Chronicle Books. She lives in Southern California.

BRADLEY OGDEN is chef and co-owner of seven San Francisco Bay Area restaurants, including the Lark Creek Inn and One Market Restaurant. Best known for his innovative use of fresh ingredients and for adding a creative edge to breakfast, he is the recipient of numerous awards and frequently appears on television and in national magazines.

LOU SEIBERT PAPPAS, as a former magazine and newspaper food editor, has written many cookbooks, among them *Biscotti; Omlettes, Frittatas, & Soufflés; Crêpes;* and *The Christmas Candy Book;* all published by Chronicle Books. She lives and teaches cooking classes in Palo Alto, California.

SARA PERRY is the author of numerous cookbooks, including *The New Complete Coffee Book, The New Tea Book, Valentine's Day Treats, Christmastime Treats, Great Gingerbread,* and *Everything Tastes Better with Bacon,* all from Chronicle Books. She lives in Portland, where she is a columnist for *The Oregonain.*

MARY S. RISLEY founded Tante Marie's Cooking School in 1973, when she left her job in investment banking to teach cooking in her San Francisco home. In 1987 she launched Food Runners, a volunteer organization that picks up excess food from businesses and delivers it to food programs, an effort that was recognized with a James Beard Foundation Humanitarian of the Year Award.

JUDY RODGERS is the James Beard Award–winning chef and co-owner of San Francisco's Zuni Café. She studied cooking in France and is a veteran of Chez Panisse and the Union Hotel, where she collaborated with Marion Cunningham. She is the author of *The Zuni Café Cookbook*.

RICK RODGERS is a well-known cookbook author, cooking teacher, and radio and television guest chef. He is the author of over twenty cookbooks including of *On Rice, Simply Shrimp, Pressure Cooking for Everyone,* and *Fried and True* (all published by Chronicle Books), as well as *Kaffeehaus*.

ELLEN ROSE founded the Cook's Library in 1989, a culinary bookstore in Los Angeles. She is a passionate cook who started collecting cookbooks at the age of seventeen. She is the author, with Jessica Strand, of *Intimate Gatherings* (Chronicle Books).

STEPHANIE ROSENBAUM is a San Francisco–based food writer and regular contributor to the *The San Francisco Bay Guardian* and *San Francisco* magazine. Her most recent book is *Honey: From Flower to Table* (Chronicle Books).

LORNA SASS is a noted authority on pressure cooking and vegan and vegetarian cooking. She writes for numerous food publications and is the author of *The New Soy Cookbook* and *The New Vegan Cookbook,* both published by Chronicle Books. She lives in New York City.

SAVEUR magazine is renowned for its coverage of authentic cooking traditions, both at home and around the world. Their cookbooks include: *Saveur Cooks Authentic American, Saveur Cooks Authentic French,* and *Saveur Cooks Authentic Italian,* all published by Chronicle Books.

BOB SLOAN is the author of *The Working Stiff Cookbook* (Chronicle Books). His mystery novels feature the homicide detective Lenny Bliss. He lives in New York City.

BRIAN ST. PIERRE reports on wine and food for *Decanter* magazine and has contributed articles to a variety of publications. He has written seven books, including *A Perfect Glass of Wine* and *The Perfect Match,* both published by Chronicle Books. He lives in London.

JESSICA STRAND is a food columnist for the *Los Angeles Times* and an avid cook. She is the author of *Intimate Gatherings* (with Ellen Rose) and *Baby's Room,* both from Chronicle Books.

DAN AND KATHLEEN TAGGART are food and wine professionals and the authors of several books including *Cooking for the Week* with Diane Morgan (Chronicle Books).

MARYANA VOLLSTEDT is the author of more than a dozen cookbooks, including *Pacific Fresh, What's For Dinner?, The Big Book of Casseroles,* and *The Big Book of Soups & Stews,* all published by Chronicle Books. She lives in Eugene, Oregon.

ROBB WALSH is the author of *Legends of Texas Barbecue Cookbook* and co-author with David Garrido of *Nuevo Tex-Mex* (both Chronicle Books), as well as a two-time James Beard Award–winner. As food critic for the *Houston Press* and commentator for National Public Radio, he has covered Texas food for more than a decade.

DIANE ROSSEN WORTHINGTON is a food writer, consultant, and James Beard Award–winning broadcaster. She is the author of fourteen books, including *The Taste of Summer, The Cuisine of California, American Bistro,* and *Seriously Simple,* all published by Chronicle Books.

JOAN ZOLOTH writes for the *Oakland Tribune*. She is a syndicated food critic for the Alameda Newspaper Group and the author of *Jewish Holiday Treats* (Chronicle Books). She lives in Northern California.

Permissions

Chicken Soup for the Soul is reprinted from *The Big Book of Soups & Stews* by Maryana Vollstedt. © 2001 by Maryana Vollstedt. Reprinted by permission of Chronicle Books.

Chicken Soup with Matzo Balls, and Beef and Barley Soup with Mushrooms are reprinted from *A Good Day for Soup* by Jeannette Ferrary and Louise Fiszer. © 1996 by Jeannette Ferrary and Louise Fiszer. Reprinted by permission of Chronicle Books.

Chicken-Coconut Soup with Galangal *(Tome Kha Gai)* is reprinted from *Real Thai* by Nancie McDermott. © 1992 by Nancie McDermott. Reprinted by permission of Chronicle Books.

Asian Chicken Noodle Soup and Couscous Salad by are reprinted from *Low-Fat Cooking to Beat the Clock* by Sam Gugino. © 2000 by Sam Gugino. Reprinted by permission of Chronicle Books.

Old-Fashioned Vegetable-Rice Soup; and Erna's Make-In-Your-Sleep Raspberry Rice Pudding are reprinted from *On Rice* by Rick Rodgers. © 1997 by Rick Rodgers. Reprinted by permission of Chronicle Books.

Minestrone Romano "a Crudo" ("Raw" Minestrone, Roman Style) is reprinted from *The Vegetarian Table: Italy* by Julia della Croce. © 1994 by Julia della Croce. Reprinted by permission of Chronicle Books.

Shiitake, Miso, and Barley Soup and Curried Tofu with Spinach and Tomatoes are reprinted from *The New Soy Cookbook* by Lorna Sass. © 1998 by Lorna J. Sass. Reprinted by permission of Chronicle Books.

Double Split Pea Soup is reprinted from *Lauren Groveman's Kitchen* by Lauren Groveman. © 1994, 2001 by Lauren Groveman. Reprinted by permission of Chronicle Books.

White Bean Soup with Winter Greens is reprinted from *Fresh from the Farmers' Market* by Janet Fletcher. © 1997 by Janet Fletcher. Reprinted by permission of Chronicle Books.

Creamy Corn Soup is reprinted from *Intimate Gatherings* by Ellen Rose and Jessica Strand. © 1998 by Ellen Rose and Jessica Strand. Reprinted by permission of Chronicle Books.

Curried Pumpkin Soup is reprinted from *Halloween Treats* by Donata Maggipinto. © 1998 by Donata Maggipinto. Reprinted by permission of Chronicle Books.

Chicken Potpies is reprinted from *Valentine Treats* by Sara Perry. © 2001 by Sara Perry. Reprinted by permission of Chronicle Books.

French Shepherd's Pie with Celery Root and Potato Topping is reprinted from *Potager* by Georgeanne Brennan. © 1992 by Georgeanne Brennan. Reprinted by permission of Chronicle Books.

Tamale Pie is reprinted from *The Supper Book* by Marion Cunningham. © 1992 by Marion Cunningham. Reprinted by permission of Alfred A. Knopf, Inc.

Italian Risotto Frittata is reprinted from *Omelettes, Soufflés & Frittatas* by Lou Seibert Pappas. © 1999 by Lou Seibert Pappas. Reprinted by permission of Chronicle Books.

Spinach and Mushroom Chilaquiles is reprinted from *Nuevo Tex-Mex* by David Garrido and Robb Walsh. © 1998 David Garrido and Robb Walsh. Reprinted by permission of Chronicle Books.

Polenta Lasagna with Tomatoes and Peppers; and Apple Crisp with Dried Fruits are reprinted from *American Bistro* by Diane Rossen Worthington. © 1997 Diane Rossen Worthington. Reprinted by permission of Chronicle Books.

Baked Eggplant Parmesan *(Melanzana alla Parmigiana)* is reprinted from *Enoteca* by Joyce Goldstein. © 2001 by Joyce Goldstein. Reprinted by permission of Chronicle Books.

Lasagna Casserole with Meat and Red Wine Sauce is reprinted from *The Pasta Book* by Julia della Croce. © Julia della Croce. Reprinted by permission of Chronicle Books.

Baked Conchiglione with Spinach-Ricotta Filling is reprinted from *Pasta Harvest* by Janet Fletcher. © 1995 by Janet Fletcher. Reprinted by permission of Chronicle Books.

Noodle Kugel is reprinted from *Jewish Holiday Treats* by Joan Zoloth. © 2000 by Joan Zoloth. Reprinted by permission of Chronicle Books.

Potato and Portobello Mushroom Casserole, Basque-Style Fisherman's Stew, Cream of Leek Soup with Stilton, and Zuni Café's Chocolate Pots de Crème are reprinted from *The San Francisco Chronicle Cookbook, Volume II* edited by Michael Bauer and Fran Irwin. © 2001 by Michael Bauer and Fran Irwin. Reprinted by permission of Chronicle Books.

Macaroni and Cheese is reprinted from *Saveur Cooks Authentic American* by the Editors of *Saveur* magazine. © 1998 by Meigher Communications, L. P. Reprinted by permission of Chronicle Books.

Roast Chicken with Lemon, Garlic, and Fresh Rosemary; and Turkey Tetrazzini are reprinted from *Cooking for the Week* by Diane Morgan, Dan Taggart, and Kathleen Taggart. © 1999 by Diane Morgan, Dan Taggart, and Kathleen Taggart. Reprinted by permission of Chronicle Books.

Chicken Simmered with Tomatoes, Fresh Herbs, and Red Wine; and Braised Lentils with Bacon are reprinted from *The San Francisco Chronicle Cookbook* edited by Michael Bauer and Fran Irwin. © 1997 by Michael Bauer and Fran Irwin. Reprinted by permission of Chronicle Books.

Classic Burgundy Beef is reprinted from *The Perfect Match* by Brian St. Pierre. © 2001 Brian St. Pierre. Reprinted by permission of Chronicle Books.

Beef Chili, is reprinted from *James McNair's Favorites* by James McNair. © 1999 by James McNair.
Reprinted by permission of Chronicle Books.

Ratatouille is reprinted from *Saveur Cooks Authentic French* by the Editors of *Saveur* magazine. © 1999 by Meigher Communications,
L. P. Reprinted by permission of Chronicle Books.

Little Meat Loaves is reprinted from *The Working Stiff Cookbook* by Bob Sloan. © 1998 by Bob Sloan.
Reprinted by permission of Chronicle Books.

Tagine of Lamb with Prunes is reprinted from *Cooking at the Kasbah* by Kitty Morse. © 1998 by Kitty Morse.
Reprinted by permission of Chronicle Books.

Baked Rigatoni with Four Cheeses is reprinted from *James McNair's Pasta Cookbook* by James McNair. Reprinted by permission of
Chronicle Books.

Mom's Meatball-Stuffed Peppers, Quick Tomato Sauce, and Gremolata are reprinted from *The Tra Vigne Cookbook* by Michael Chiarello
with Penelope Wisner. © 1999 by Michael Chiarello. Reprinted by permission of Chronicle Books.

Tailgate Potato Salad is reprinted from *Potato Salad* by Barbara Lauterbach. © 2002 by Barbara Lauterbach.
Reprinted by permission of Chronicle Books.

Green Bean Salad with Yellow Pepper, Jicama, and Tomato is reprinted from *The Taste of Summer* by Diane Rossen Worthington.
© 2000 Diane Rossen Worthington. Reprinted by permission of Chronicle books.

Caramelized Roasted Vegetables is reprinted from *Olive Oil* by Peggy Knickerbocker. © 1997 by Peggy Knickerbocker.
Reprinted by permission of Chronicle Books.

Autumn Rice with Red Peppers and Pine Nuts is reprinted from *The Cuisine of California* by Diane Rossen Worthington. © 1983,
1997 by Diane Rossen Worthington. Reprinted by permission of Chronicle Books.

Soba Noodle Salad with Tamari Dressing is reprinted from *Dean & DeLuca: The Food and Wine Cookbook* by Jeff Morgan. © 2002 by
Jeff Morgan. Reprinted by permission of Chronicle Books.

Warm Moroccan Beet Salad with Tangerines; and Chocolate Bread Pudding with Sun-Dried Cherries are reprinted from
The Secrets of Success Cookbook by Michael Bauer. © 2000 by Michael Bauer. Reprinted by permission of Chronicle Books.

Butterscotch Pudding; and Double-Fudge Frosted Brownies are reprinted from *Diner Desserts* by Tish Boyle. © 2000 by Tish Boyle.
Reprinted by permission of Chronicle Books.

Buttery Pound Cake is reprinted from *James McNair's Cakes* by James McNair. © 1999 by James McNair.
Reprinted by permission of Chronicle Books.

Glazed Cinnamon Rolls is reprinted from *The Bread Bible* by Beth Hensperger. © 1999 by Beth Hensperger.
Reprinted by permission of Chronicle Books.

Index

Table of Equivalents

THE EXACT EQUIVALENTS IN THE FOLLOWING TABLES HAVE BEEN ROUNDED FOR CONVENIENCE.

US/UK

oz = ounce
lb = pound
in = inch
ft = foot
tbl = tablespoon
fl oz = fluid ounce
qt = quart

METRIC

g = gram
kg = kilogram
mm = millimeter
cm = centimeter
ml = milliliter
l = liter

LENGTH MEASURES

⅛ in	3 mm
¼ in	6 mm
½ in	12 mm
1 in	2.5 cm
2 in	5 cm
3 in	7.5 cm
4 in	10 cm
5 in	13 cm
6 in	15 cm
7 in	18 cm
8 in	20 cm
9 in	23 cm
10 in	25 cm
11 in	28 cm
12/1 ft	30 cm

WEIGHTS

US/UK	Metric
1 oz	30 g
2 oz	60 g
3 oz	90 g
4 oz (¼ lb)	125 g
5 oz (⅓ lb)	155 g
6 oz	185 g
7 oz	220 g
8 oz (½ lb)	250 g
10 oz	315 g
12 oz (¾ lb)	375 g
14 oz	440 g
16 oz (1 lb)	500 g
1½ lb	750 g
2 lb	1 kg
3 lb	1.5 kg

OVEN TEMPERATURES

Fahrenheit	Celsius	Gas
250	120	½
275	140	1
300	150	2
325	160	3
350	180	4
375	190	5
400	200	6
425	220	7
450	230	8
475	240	9
500	260	10

LIQUIDS

US	Metric	UK
2 tbl	30 ml	1 fl oz
¼ cup	60 ml	2 fl oz
⅓ cup	80 ml	3 fl oz
½ cup	125 ml	4 fl oz
⅔ cup	160 ml	5 fl oz
¾ cup	180 ml	6 fl oz
1 cup	250 ml	8 fl oz
1½ cups	375 ml	12 fl oz
2 cups	500 ml	16 fl oz
4 cups/1 qt	1 l	32 fl oz